R.P.M.
REALIZE YOUR
POWER TO
MOTIVATE

R.P.M.
REALIZE YOUR
POWER TO
MOTIVATE

Mary Sanders
and
Elizabeth Field

Edited by Jan Urban-Lurain
Cover Design & Illustrations
by Kent Ver Planck

Milestones Unlimited
A Productivity Development Company
Suite 105
35552 Grand River Avenue
Farmington Hills, Michigan 48024

R.P.M.
REALIZE YOUR POWER TO MOTIVATE

Dedicated to Mary A. Hayes, Dr.William D. Sanders, Mable J. French, and to Motivators who have a mission of motivating, helping, influencing and inspiring. They have made and will continue to make a difference in the lives of many.

Acknowledgments

We wish to thank the many people who have helped us during this process of writing and publishing this book.

Foremost, we wish to thank Jan Urban-Lurain for using her limited personal time to edit the many versions of this book. She not only fulfilled the role of editor but, from the very beginning encouraged us to make this a book of hope and help to those who read it. At several critical points, she gently pushed us in new directions of analysis.

We wish to thank Jackie Lichty for her countless hours of support and suggestions. Her encouragement and inspiration has motivated the authors when we needed it most. Her nurturing efforts of providing food and coffee were gratefully accepted during final crunch periods.

We appreciated Mark Urban-Lurain's thoughtful assistance and analysis in developing our research questionnaire.

We sincerely appreciate the editing and warm comments of those who reviewed the text prior to final editing. Thank you Margaret Bucklin, Pam Czuj, Ruth Martens, Les McClelland, and Judy McQueen for giving us honest feedback.

The efforts of Louise Coleman throughout the final stages of preparation for publication were tirelessly given and sincerely appreciated. In addition, Bob Coleman and Louise Coleman assisted us in final proofing efforts during a critical period while we were concentrating on other final details.

We also wish to thank the numerous individuals who contributed their thoughts and energy during our research stages. Among these individuals are

Debbie Aho, Ronna Hoffmann-Albers, Barbara Bliss, Karen Boland, Margaret Bucklin, Pam Czuj, Dr. Harold Ellens, Susan Garrity, John Green, Charles Harstead, Olga Holden, Marilyn French Hubbard, Rea Kennedy, Jackie Lichty, Mary Lee Lord, Joseph Mendez, Les McClelland, Judy McQueen, Floyd Oursler, Sandy Parker, Jane Rhodes, Sister Madeline Sage, Ellen Sanders, Dr. Douglas Sanders, Helen Schwartz, Harold Taylor, Joan Tirak, and Kent Ver Planck.

As always we wish to thank our parents and family for their support of our efforts. These people have consistently and tirelessly given of their love and caring to us over the years. With their motivational energy and inspirational guidance, we have obtained the basis of the philosophies expressed within this book. Even if "you can't go home again," it's nice to know they are with us where ever we go.

Finally we wish to thank our seminar participants and college students who have encouraged us by letting us know the concepts and suggestions we have to offer have been of practical help for them.

CONTENTS

SECTION A:
THE POWER TO MOTIVATE

SECTION B:
THE POWER DRAIN

SECTION C: REVVING UP YOUR POWER TO MOTIVATE AS A MANAGER

SECTION A:
THE POWER TO MOTIVATE

A-1
WHAT SPARKS YOUR MOTIVATION?

"'Where do you get the energy?' she asked me. I don't really know. An idea just comes, and I'm off and running. I love to see an idea become reality." (Motivation for this author is energy.)

"Where do you get the motivation?" seems to be a pertinent question to people who don't have it or want more, especially when they see others who have it and use it.

When people ask where do you get the motivation. They really want to know two things: What is it? and How do I get it?

It's difficult to define motivation because it's an intangible and it can be an observable effect, a quality, a power or an energy or all of these.

Motivation is definitely infectious. The power of motivation can quickly spread between people. A motivated person can energize others if they have a desire to be motivated.

Where do you get your energy? Where do you get the motivation? Is motivation an end or a beginning? How do you get more of it? How do you motivate others as a leader or manager? How do you create a productive and motivated team? These are just some of the questions we will be examining throughout the book.

OUR SECRETS

For years, theorists have been trying to explain motivation and how people are motivated. None of these theories or definitions truly define the nature and essence of motivation. Although we recognize the value of these and other motivation theories, we question whether any one theory can truly capture all the many nuances of motivation.

We are not about to say it is beyond definition, however, perhaps the premises which others have previously used were slightly skewed to their thought processes. Quite naturally ours will be too.

We are not going to propose a new theory of motivation to you in this book. Instead a definition and description of motivation is provided as we have perceived it from our research and experiences.

When we began to examine the secrets of motivation, we realized that the term motivation is used to explain many different situations.

You can see the results and the effects on the person who is motivated. The reasons for motivation as the theorists have described it are varied because there are different types of people and motives. Some theorists have tried to quantify motivation. They have avoided revealing a more ethereal premise that motivation is truly an energy that spontaneously occurs for a myriad of reasons chosen by the person who feels this energy.

Our premise suggests that motivation is an energy source. This energy creates a liveliness that invigorates you to do, create, perform and act in a diligent manner. The energy originates within you when you are stimulated by any one of three sources: yourself, others or a situation. The motivational energy originates with ideas, desires, needs, or for the sheer joy of being and doing. Others can set up circumstances or pose questions which motivate you. Likewise motivation can be the answer to a pressing need. Prior to energy release, however, you must perceive the task or activity to be worthy of your attention and action.

THE THEORISTS SAY...

Motive is defined by Webster's New World Dictionary as "an inner drive, an impulse, or something that causes one to act." The verb to motivate is defined by the American Heritage Dictionary as "to stimulate to action; to provide with an incentive or motive; impel; incite."

But what really is motivation? Theorists such as Abraham Maslow and others suggest that we are motivated by unfilled needs. An unfilled need creates a vacuum of desire. Maslow perceived five different levels of needs: physical, security and safety, social, self esteem, and self actualization. When a need level isn't fulfilled, a person concentrates on that set of needs until it is fulfilled.

Victor Vroom developed an equation for motivation. This equation essentially proposes that the strength of someone's motivation is a combination of: 1) the perceived value of the result of performing a behavior and 2) the perceived probability that the result will occur. As these two factors increase in value, the person's motivation increases. If you perceive that you will gain a tremendous amount of prestige from one activity and that you will be successful in performing the activity, then you will be highly motivated to perform the activity.

David McClelland proposed that people are motivated by high and low needs for achievement. Those who have a high need will set goals that are challenging and realistic. Those who have a low need for achievement tend to avoid challenges and risks.

Others have theorized that internal motivation and external motivation drive people. External motivation relates to rewards from outside influences. Internal motivators are personal rewards the person gives to himself or herself.

L. W. Porter and E. E. Lawler developed a model that combines the best of some of these ideas. Their model suggests that a person is motivated by the perceived value of intrinsic and extrinsic rewards for performing an effort and whether these are fair rewards for the effort. They also suggest that actual performance will be affected not only by the person's perception of what is needed to do the task but also by the person's ability to accomplish the task. They also propose that satisfaction from the rewards will spur similar behavior.

YOU HAVE THE POWER TO MOTIVATE

You have the power to motivate yourself and to motivate others. Indeed, everyone has the ability to realize the power to motivate. Motivation is a power or an energy source, that you can create. If you have the power to motivate, you are plugged into an energy source that can stimulate you and others.

By and large, the vast majority of us seem to be unaware of our power to be and to do the most we are capable of being and doing. We tend to understate our potential even to ourselves. Unfortunately, some of us lack either the motivation or the person who can help us become motivated. What a waste! Each of us has a great potential to learn, grow and become in this life.

You can be the motivational force behind your energy momentum. Why wait for it to come from others? It's there inside you, waiting to be released. Be the stimulus instead of waiting for a stimulus to get you in the mood. Be in control of your present destiny by taking charge of this very moment and deciding you are motivated to become all that you can be.

A-2
FIND OUT
WHO HAS THE
POWER TO
MOTIVATE

WHO ARE THESE PEOPLE?

John is a manager, who loves to work with people. Frequently people tell him how much he has inspired them. They are ready to move ahead in a new direction because of his belief in them and his verbal encouragement.

Others admire Celeste for her ability and drive. If she has a goal, watch out. She's going after it. She will sacrifice personal needs for the need of the moment which is to reach that goal. Some people find themselves challenged by her. She motivates by both her behavior and by her encouraging positive messages.

Paul works all day and 3/4 of the night and is right back at it the next morning at 6. He never seems to tire. He only laughs when you suggest slowing down. He enjoys his work more than any other part of his life.

Tracey is in a helping profession, where the needs are great and few people can adequately do the job. She is a giving person, who has chosen to help others through her work. She burned out a few years ago because the work sapped her mental, psychological and physical energy. Yet, she keeps on giving.

Who are these unique people who as hard workers, give, motivate, influence and inspire others?

They are the Motivators. They have the power to motivate and frequently use it. They work in different types of organizations and create amazing results by their motivational power. Though their professions are very different, they have many common character traits.

THE ELEMENTS OF THE MOTIVATOR CHARACTER

What are the common elements of a Motivator's character and behaviors that make them so special? Through our research, we have found they possess these qualities and characteristics.

- Givers, who have life time goals of helping others
- Self Confident
- Keen Analytical Abilities
- Theoretical and Practical Intelligence that is quickly applied to problem solving
- Strong Intuitive Abilities
- Perceptive and Insightful about their own and others' strengths and weaknesses
- Sensitive to Others' Needs
- Effective Listening Abilities
- Slightly Dramatic
- Capable of developing their own inner characters
- Influence, inspire and motivate others to action
- Ambitious
- Perseverant and Persistent
- Personable
- Very seldom boring or bored
- Articulate, both verbally and nonverbally
- Slightly Impatient because they want to move on
- Remarkable Ability to appreciate and accentuate the highs in life
- Hard Working
- Finishers of what they start
- Able to see and enjoy the Humorous side of life
- Initiate many projects (Often more than they can physically accomplish)
- Self Accepting if they are healthy Motivators
- May be self destructive because some tend to magnify their weaknesses
- Like to read...they are Continual Learners...typically read more than the average person
- Creative
- Lead others by using words, their inspirational voice qualities and by their actions
- Have a sense of responsibility for commitments and for others' welfare and ultimate good
- May be official or unofficial mentors
- Enjoy seeing others grow, achieve and learn

Although each Motivator is an individual with strengths and flaws, we have found that most Motivators have these common qualities.

Most successful organizations have a least one Motivator in every functional area. However, the massive impact of these people reaches far beyond the organizational limits of profits, products and services.

RARE BREED OF PEOPLE: PEOPLE WITH A MISSION

Motivators are set apart from the rest of their culture. They are like the scouts of the old west. They are sent ahead of the culture to translate, to motivate, and to influence. They couldn't depart from these roles even if they wanted to because being a Motivator is an essential life function. For many, being a Motivator is also a life long occupation. They typically don't retire from it, which is exciting for most of them because they are never cut off from their life's love.

They are probably born with a mission and even as children they seem to have something different that sets them apart from others. As children they are often hard workers. They tend to stand out from the rest of the crowd. Their parents and grandparents indoctrinated them with the belief system that work gives meaning to their lives. Although many detested household and/or farm chores as children, strangely those very experiences seem to have embedded within them a positive view of hard work.

If there is a grand plan in various fields and aspects of life, the Motivators are the leaders. They are sent to do something different and to help the people they meet to be a part of the plan. It may not be religious but it is probably somewhat spiritual because they develop other's hidden talents to their full potential. They help Motivators, nonMotivators and followers. Certainly, they are a different breed of people who stand out in the history of organizations.

Motivators have purposes or missions to carry out in this life. Some have a very specific idea of what this mission is, while others are continually discovering new facets of it. Still others seem to finish one mission and then choose another to complete.

How do they perceive their missions in terms of living their lives? One Motivator commented, "The mission can be a lonely road to follow. Once you believe you have a mission or purpose in life, you have accepted a tremendous responsibility to live out that mission(s). You also come to realize there are aspects of life that you must forgo to accomplish that mission."

Another Motivator discussed the preceeding aspects thusly: "The Frost poem's line of 'I have many miles to go before I sleep' relates to the endurance and purposefulness of the Motivator. We have to touch a lot of lives. We don't know the shortness of our life spans. Even if we lived until 120, it would still be important to do much with this moment in time and to accomplish everything possible in a life time.

Most of us probably have several life time missions. These change as the years go by. Some goals are more likely general directions rather than specific objectives."

When asked about the development of her sense of mission, one Motivator commented…"I remember taking world history in high school. For the first time, I realized how insignificant one person is when compared to all of the civilizations that had risen and fallen. Everybody who had lived and died had just been forgotten. I went through a tremendous sense of depression and I can remember having a discussion with my history teacher. I told him how overwhelmed and just totally awful I felt about having come to this conclusion. He said, 'it's not so much what's written down in history or whether people remember you or not, it's the people whose lives you touch in your immediate surroundings as you go through life that you make the difference in a life.'" Truly, Motivators make a difference in the lives around them. Most of it is not of historical significance but for the person who has been changed by a Motivator's influence, the result is not forgotten.

The word mission, which means "a sending out or being sent out to perform a special duty" carries with it a tremendous weight of life's purpose with it. We found most Motivators either desirous to discover it or to fulfill it. For example, one Motivator revealed her sense of mission. "There is a grand design to this whole process. I'm not sure I have a handle on what it is. I perceive myself to be a leader now and I never used to. I rejected the idea of leadership in the past. My mission in life before I die....what I want to accomplish is to help someone who lacks confidence. This would be one who really is very talented but who's self confidence is so bad that they don't recognize it and one who given enough, could do something really phenomenonal.'"

We also found Motivators to be extremely confident in their roles. Although each has a source of power, for most it's enough just to know they have it. They seldom find the need to exercise it.

Many times Motivators motivate by behavior as well as words. Their lives are perfect examples of making life count for something. Their enthusiasm is often contagious to their followers. Most of the time, they seem to be in tune with the needs of the people they are motivating. A true Motivator seems to only asks followers to do things, she/he is willing to do herself or himself. Frequently, the Motivator is in there pitching with the followers to make a project a success. This type of behavior promotes a tremendous amount of loyalty to the Motivator, as you can well imagine.

Motivators are an elite group. The market demand for their talents is huge, but few people seem to fill the position with this special temperment.

THE EFFECTS OF THE MISSION AS A MESSAGE

Motivators, who don't have a full complement of self confidence develop it through the propagation of their mission. They even begin to believe their messages. This is especially true for the Motivators, who are ministers, public speakers and trainers. As they state their messages, they discover they need to hear it as much as their audiences. So they continually reinforce their messages for themselves.

A true Motivator communicates basic truths that tend to haunt you long after the words have been spoken. One thoughtful Motivator commented about this element by saying "The message digs deep into your heart and won't let go until you've dealt with it. Some times a person's life is permanently altered by just a few well chosen words."

THE REAL GIVERS

Motivators love to give to others. They give for many different reasons. Some Motivators give because of their missions, which they discovered early in life. Others give because they didn't learn to love themselves so they try to make up for it by loving others. In their own way, they may be trying to earn love and self respect by producing it in others. The problem with this approach is that it doesn't work for the long run. When the Motivator leaves the stage of performance or is forced to leave, the Motivator doesn't continue to feel the same sense of self esteem. Still, others give from a strong base of self esteem and self confidence. Some give because they enjoy seeing others profit, thus these Motivators gain a tremendous amount of self satisfaction.

MOTIVATED BY THEIR PASSIONS

Work is one of the Motivator's major passions. Their sense of self esteem seems to be inextricably linked with their work or mission. One Motivator told us, "If we're not working, we're not living. We are less than we should be if we are not accepting our mission." Motivators need to feel they are doing and being their best most of the time. Having strong desires and capacities to live up to their full potential, work must have meaning for them. Work and seeing the results of their work increases their sense of self esteem.

Some Motivators seem to be saying with their actions, "to do less is to be less."

They enjoy work immensely and probably most of the facets of their work. Work is like a glove that when put on, it fits quite comfortably. Indeed, their personality characteristics and their choice of work are a perfect match.

One executive we interviewed said "I enjoy the creativity and excitement of it. I like to see things grow. I don't do it for the money. I just find that life's meant to be creative in certain ways. If you just go to a job and you come home and enjoy yourself and buy the boats, houses, cars and vacations, life loses a lot of meaning."

Motivators seem to choose their work consciously and subconsciously. By working, their hidden skills are brought out. They tend to see their work positively because they can see the results of their labors. Often they see magnificent changes in others' attitudes and behaviors.

HOW THEY VIEW WORK

Work is a major passion of their lives. They love it. They find it fun, pleasurable and thrilling. Some even equated work with life. One called it an euphoric and anesthesia. Motivators want to do their best while working.

"Work gives me purpose," one very competent manager told us. "I love to have fun and I love to play but I feel that you can do that while you work. I'm a person who I think tends to be a little bit too serious in terms of her work. I have a strong sense of integrity and a strong sense of value and what ever I do I like to do well...I'm not a perfectionist. I feel that we're all human and nobody is perfect but I strive for excellence and I strive for doing a good job at what I do."

One Motivator talked about the ironical side of work, "a true definition of work encompasses life. Life is work. You're exchanging your life for doing things which depending on whether you enjoy it or not may be hard work or not considered work." Most Motivators love their work. Some love it too much.

A sales Motivator described her love hate relationship with work by saying, "It's a euphoric and an anesthesia. I've had the most exhilarating highs over work and the accomplishment connected with work at the emotional level of anything I've ever had. I also know work is for me a pain avoider." She continues to discuss how when she encountered a personal disappointment, she would fill her time with more work to make up for it.

Dr. Harold Ellens shared his thoughts from a philosophical point of view. He said, "For me, work is creating and caring for people. Everything that I do is really consciously a process of caring for people in creative ways and creating insights regarding the nature and meaning for caring for people. . .

I think what drives me, as the central driver, is that the conviction that everything in the end comes down to aesthetics. That the whole enterprise of human motivation is moved by the innate sense that we exist for the purpose of seeking and celebrating and preserving the good, the true and the beautiful. One thing has always been absolutely centrally clear to me and that is that I was always moving consistently in one direction and that is toward aesthetic idealism, toward the enhancement of beauty and goodness and truth in human experience."

To say work is important to the Motivator is an understatement. As we've said many see it as life giving. They never see themselves without some kind of work. Certainly their early influences such as role models impacted their feelings about work. Most Motivators love to work. They find it gives them meaning as well as pleasure. A portion of their social activities are provided by their work relationships. It does far more than just occupy their time and provide an economic security blanket. Their work provides purpose for living. Their work is the fulfillment of their mission.

On a slightly humorous vein, one Motivator described work as "shit." With a serious explanation, she stated, "I think work is getting down into the nitty gritty, sort of getting down in the dirt and into it and really mucking around and if you don't get down into it then it's not work.   Probably everything I do in my life is work. I really think my life is work and work is life."

Even for the Motivator, work is a two sided coin. It has a life giving, creative and fun side. It also has a side that is disciplined, detailed and commitment side. Neither of which are bad but one is often the result of desiring to have more of the other.

PASSION SOMETIMES LEADS TO COMPULSION

Motivators are people who are the 110% givers and can be fast burn out victims. Later in the book, we discuss work behaviors that can be truly harmful to Motivators. Their passion to give and achieve can sometimes lead to compulsive behavior. For all the good they do, their own personal lives sometimes suffer.

STRONG SENSE OF INDEPENDENCE

Motivators have a tremendous ability to be self confident and independent. They express this self confidence by verbalizing and acting in ways other people wouldn't dream of. They have noticed the rest of the population is different from them but their strong sense of independence and confidence allows them to continue to be as they are. They know who is in control of their lives...them, not others. This is probably one of the more unusual facts about them. They are influenced somewhat by others but typically they do what they want to do in a society that often encourages and pressures people to be similar. Peer pressure seems to have no more effect than a nasty mosquito buzzing. Motivators confidently know where they are heading and are able to keep going despite these peer pressures.

MOVING FORWARD IN THE FAST LANE

When other people compare their activity and energy levels with the Motivator, they have mixed reactions. Motivators are very different from the average person, who goes to work each day for eight hours. They are extremely hard working and professional no matter how many hours they actually work. Many perceive themselves as hard working, some as much as 12-18 hours/day. Strangely, some Motivators typically think their behavior is average or at least nothing special.

One Motivator still remains mystified by others' responses. "People say 'Wow! You've really accomplished a lot for your age. How do you get it all done?' When I look at my achievements, I wish I could do more. In fact, I often feel slow or behind in many areas of life."

Most of the Motivators indicated that they have high energy levels, frequently thinking of numerous ideas and goals to accomplish, and are constantly doing. They seem to have far more energy and ideas than their peers. Some even told us that others are worn out by their high energy levels. Some of these Motivators think fast, talk fast, work fast, and move fast. Compared to their friends, associates, acquaintances and family, their schedules seem overwhelmingly full.

We found Motivators are always busy and typically complaining about being busy. Their comments range from "It's just crazy" to "I'm out of control."

Other statements include...

> "I feel like a one legged man in an ass kicking contest."
> "I'm having one of those days."
> "I feel like I'm being pulled in a million directions today."

Usually it's said in a humorously negative manner. They seem to being saying "Oh, isn't it awful!" The truth is they wouldn't have it any other way. If you ask them to stop or slow down, you'll get every rationale in the book of why they can't, even though they probably could somewhat.

Some of the Motivator's friends and spouses undoubtedly feel they have their Motivator's best interests at heart when suggesting slowing down. While others may be acting unwittingly from envy, however the desired effect of the Motivator reducing his/her speed is seldom accomplished. Whether the Motivator should slow down or not is a matter each person must decide for himself or herself. One fact is certain, the Motivator is typically a go getter who has got up and gone after what he or she wants in life.

One Motivator in an executive position exemplified this by stating "I think of ideas for change and it frightens some. I believe people who are looking through the front of the windshield don't get worn out. Other people look in the rear view mirror too often and it wears the hell out of them."

Surprisingly, for their rapid pace of work, most of the Motivators never expect others to be able to fully keep up with them. They just expect others to try. Based upon the continuing suggestions to take it easy or slow down, we have concluded that many times Motivators haven't communicated this perspective effectively to their associates. Many Motivators have talked about their fast paced life to receive praise, only to receive the "slow down" advice. Sometimes these associates are responding from their own feelings of guilt or inadequacy to keep up with the Motivator. Although much of the advice is well intentioned, the Motivators' zest for life in the fast lane creates an ironical situation, which we will discuss in greater detail later in the book regarding the the work addiction cycle and work compulsion.

THE MOTIVES BEHIND THE MOTIVATOR

Many Motivators have the desire to do something positive for the world. If they see an opportunity, they respond to it. Some are even considered visionaries. Their purpose in life is one of serving people.

They believe in their talents and abilities. Usually others will comment about their self confidence. This self confidence gives them the energy to complete their missions.

They want to see their messages live on and on. They experience the tremendous thrill of seeing people they have inspired go on to influence other people. They relish a secret satisfaction of knowing they started the momentum.   Motivators get a tremendous thrill from presenting to or leading groups.

One educator, Joan Tirak commented, "teaching seems to be a place where we can meet people where they are, at their own level of work and help them to move beyond that stage to something else. I've learned that I can really touch people on a grass roots level where they need to be touched."

They are also motivated by the responses of those they motivate. Amazingly in an age when people are secretly begging for appreciation, they are often thanked for what they do. They are highly regarded by peers and superiors in their companies and organizations. The appreciation can cause them to do even more.

The world around Motivators excites them. They are motivated by the excitement of living and learning from positive and negative experiences. As truly positive people, they tend to interpret most situations from a positive perspective.

FOREVER LEARNING TO TEACH

As continual learners, Motivators are constantly being consumers of education and current events. Most enjoy reading and tend to read and summarize for other people. They are often purveyors of knowledge. Some like to communicate sophisticated information they learn in a practical and applicable format for their listeners.

As Karen Boland, a public speaker explained it, "These are ideas that help change peoples' lives and that is of great interest to me. Because my life has been changed by these ideas. Having learned by them and worked with them, it's now my opportunity to give back those ideas."

LIFE TRANSLATES TO APPLICATION

They frequently are translating other experiences to their work. When watching real life drama or a television drama, they are thinking about how they can apply the information to their own or others' experiences.

Most Motivators do not have a natural ability to turn off their minds. They are constantly working on a concept or idea. They have to consciously try to redirect their minds. The nature of their work frequently requires them to perform new tasks and solve problems thus they try to find meaning in everything and then apply the ideas to their work. They are usually making applications during play too. Everything in life becomes part of the material they can draw upon. Life becomes an amalgamation of work.

They may use what they learn to teach others. The salesperson may be thinking of how he would sell a product while watching a commercial. The executive sees a new project by driving in the country and observing nature. The teacher or trainer observes something that he/she can use with students or participants. This natural ability helps them to be highly creative individuals.

SELF ACTUALIZED PEOPLE...

If we were to integrate the Motivator concept with Maslow's Hierarchy of Needs, where would most Motivators find themselves? On Maslow's Hierarchy of Needs, they are usually on the fourth and fifth levels of fulfilling self esteem and self actualization needs. They tend to be self actualized individuals or very close to being. They understand themselves fairly well and are not afraid to keep learning about themselves. Typically, Motivators understand their motives for behaving the way they do. Given a strong base of self esteem, healthy Motivators are able to give to others from a bountiful store. One commented that she was willing to give till it hurt but not in a long term self sacrificing manner. Motivators truly have the best interests of others at heart when they give, motivate, and influence.

WHAT ABOUT YOU?

Perhaps you're wondering if you are a Motivator? To give you an opportunity to determine if you are, we have developed the Motivator Characteristic Quiz.

MOTIVATOR CHARACTERISTIC QUIZ

To the left of each statement, circle SD if you strongly disagree with the statement, circle D if you disagree with it, circle N if you neither agree or disagree with it, circle A if you agree with it, circle SA if you strongly agree with it.

1. **I ENJOY WORKING**	SD D N A SA
2. **I ENJOY WORKING IMMENSELY**	SD D N A SA
3. **I HAVE STRONG LEADERSHIP CAPABILITIES**	SD D N A SA
4. **I ENJOY INFLUENCING OTHER'S BEHAVIOR**	SD D N A SA
5. **I HAVE FOUND GREAT REWARDS IN WORKING HARD**	SD D N A SA
6. **I AM HAPPIEST WHEN I'M WORKING ON SOMETHING THAT GIVES MEANING TO LIFE**	SD D N A SA
7. **I PLAY AS HARD AS I WORK**	SD D N A SA
8. **MY WORK INVOLVES HELPING OTHERS**	SD D N A SA
9. **SOMETIMES, I THINK I INSPIRE OTHERS**	SD D N A SA
10. **PEOPLE ARE AMAZED AT HOW MUCH I AM ABLE TO ACCOMPLISH**	SD D N A SA
11. **PEOPLE HAVE COMMENTED THAT I AM AN ENTHUSIASTIC PERSON**	SD D N A SA

12. I HAVE MORE WORK IDEAS THAN I
    HAVE TIME TO DO THEM   SD D N A SA

13. I AM A PERSON WHO PUSHES AND
    DRIVES MYSELF TO EXCELLENCE   SD D N A SA

14. I SEEK PERFECTION IN MOST OF
    MY WORK   SD D N A SA

15. I BELIEVE I CAN ALWAYS DO BETTER   SD D N A SA

16. I BELIEVE I AM MORE COMPETENT
    THAN THE MAJORITY OF PEOPLE
    IN MY PROFESSION   SD D N A SA

17. I EXPECT MORE OF MYSELF THAN
    OTHERS DO   SD D N A SA

18. I EXPECT MORE FROM OTHERS THAN
    THEY ARE USUALLY WILLING TO GIVE   SD D N A SA

19. I FIND WORK STIMULATING   SD D N A SA

20. MY WORK RELATES TO A MISSION OR
    PURPOSE I HAVE IN LIFE   SD D N A SA

21. MY WORK IS ALTRUISTIC   SD D N A SA

22. IF I WON THE LOTTERY, I WOULD
    CONTINUE IN MY PRESENT WORK   SD D N A SA

23. I KNOW WHEN I HAVE DONE A GOOD JOB   SD D N A SA

24. I HAVE A HEALTHY EGO   SD D N A SA

25. I HAVE SOMETHING SPECIAL
    TO OFFER OTHERS   SD D N A SA

26. I LIKE BEING BY MYSELF   SD D N A SA

27. I ENJOY WORKING WITH OTHERS   SD D N A SA

28. I AM USUALLY VERY PRODUCTIVE   SD D N A SA

29. I AM A GOOD LISTENER   SD D N A SA

30. I AM ABLE TO LISTEN AND PERCEIVE
    OTHERS NEEDS   SD D N A SA

31. I USE MANY PROBING QUESTIONS WHEN
    COMMUNICATING ON THE JOB   SD D N A SA

32. I USE MANY PROBING QUESTIONS WHEN
    COMMUNICATING OFF THE JOB   SD D N A SA

33. I HAVE AN EQUAL BALANCE OF TIME
    BETWEEN WORK AND OTHER ACTIVITIES   SD D N A SA

34. MY WORK IS MY LIFE'S GREATEST FOCUS   SD D N A SA

WHAT CHARACTERISTICS/QUALITIES DO YOUR FRIENDS HAVE?

WHAT CHARACTERISTICS/ QUALITIES DO THOSE YOU RESPECT HAVE?

IF YOU COULD BE AN ANIMAL, WHAT WOULD YOU BE AND WHY?

For questions 1-34, if you put...
SD, give yourself one point
D, give yourself two points
N, give yourself three points
A, give yourself four points
SA, give yourself five points
If you scored between 34-50, most likely you're not a Motivator.
If you scored between 51-102, you have potential. To become one, you have your work cut out for you.
If you scored between 103-136, you're most likely a Motivator.
If you scored between 137-170, you're most definitely a Motivator.

Take a look at what you answered for questions 35 and 36, are the characteristics and qualities you listed, Motivator characteristics? Do you emulate these qualities?

Why did you choose the animal you did? What does it tell you about your views and behaviors?

If you think you're a Motivator, welcome to the club. You are a unique person, who has much to give and far to go. As a Motivator you have the power to motivate yourself and others. This book is written to help you.

If you don't fit the mold, be happy with who you are and become all you can be. You probably have much to offer. Everyone has the potential to become a Motivator. If you wish to become a Motivator or to understand them, read on.

A-3
WHAT IS THE MOTIVATOR'S WORK VEHICLE?

Motivators are truly unique individuals who enjoy and thrive on working with people. Naturally, they work in occupations that allow them to use these skills. Although the functional areas differ, most Motivators spend the majority of their hours working, communicating and just being with people. To give you the flavor of what the Motivator's work is like, we want to share some of their perspectives of work and why they are in the professions they chose.

An interesting point to note about Motivators is that while many of them knew at an early age what they would be, several told us their work seemed to choose them. In particular, one Motivator indicated that it was a result of growing up in the 60's as well as fate to a certain extent, which determined her career direction and upward movement. Another mentioned it was an economic necessity to work outside the home so she chose something she would enjoy.

Motivators work in many different occupations and professions. You never know when or where you'll meet one.

THE VEEPS, ADMINISTRATORS, EXECUTIVE DIRECTORS AND PRESIDENTS

Many Motivators work in the upper echelons of corporations and organizations. Amazingly, some of these Motivators tend to think of themselves in terms of being entrepreneurs. They see the challenges of their jobs as opportunities to create new solutions and new ideas. They frequently mentioned how much they enjoyed their work. Philosophically for some, their reasons for enjoyment were expressed in terms of humanitarianism. Others described it more in terms of personal satisfaction.

A common type of response from executive Motivators is exemplified by the statement made by this Motivator, "I thoroughly enjoy work. I get up in the morning and I think of what can we do differently...how can we do it better...I don't just mean just what can we do as a company or a division but also what can we do as people. How can we do something that will make the company better, create more jobs, have more fun, just the whole process."

In addition to work being enjoyable, most Motivators expressed the need for self satisfaction similar to the comments by this sales executive, "I am in my profession because of the charge I get out of it. I enjoy seeing different people...challenging to meet the people I work with. I guess the bottom line is satisfaction. You get a satisfaction...a personal satisfaction from it. I have always held that income is second to being happy in what you're doing."

An executive director of a human services agency explained how and why she was in her career by saying..."I didn't really understand what I was choosing. I like working with people, I like to talk to people, talk with people and listen to them and I think they're fascinating. I'd much prefer interaction with people than I do computers, machines or paper. The way people decide to handle their lives is fascinating. The choices they make. I think I'm learning how people handle things, how they adapt. It's incredible to me how diversified we are as a species."

Others see themselves in terms of being humanitarians, as these two Motivators, who describe the reasons for being in their professions. Marilyn Hubbard, a professional training consultant said "I found my niche, it lets me do everything I want to do and it helps me to do things that I wanted to do for the world and do the things I need to do for myself." Another Motivator commented..."My basic philosophy and makeup is one of a humanitarian. I've always been directed toward elements of teaching."

These types of Motivators are true givers. When they see a need, they desire to fill it. It's almost as if they hate to see vacuums. Certainly, the vacuum creates a need within them to fill it. The needs they fill are usually marketable and they are able to enjoy the monetary profits as well as the psychological profits.

Companies and organizations with Motivators at their helms are in an advantageous position in the competition. Motivators, who are motivated and extremely capable in motivating others are the essential elements of excellent companies. It's a well known fact that successful changes must start at the top of the organization. Motivators in these positions tend to be tremendous agents for positive change.

TRAINERS, TEACHERS AND PROFESSORS

Like executives, this group of professional trainers and educators see themselves and their occupations as a means of accomplishing a particular mission, while enjoying the process. This group in particular is process oriented because often the results of their mission are not apparent for many years. So they concentrate on the momentary achievements. They gain tremendous highs from the process of watching the impact of their messages upon their students, trainees or participants. Most enjoy the process of communicating.

Joan Tirak commented about teaching…"teaching is the best way to contact people at a basic level of formation. There aren't enough teachers to help us understand what's appropriate pain and what's inappropriate pain and what to capitalize on in life and learn from others' experiences." Being people oriented, Motivators love to influence others in positive manners. They seem to know just how much to say and the best way to say it.

A trainer indicated her reasons thusly…"my mission is to help others. I want to make a difference. My goal is to leave behind products that will benefit people who live after me. These become the symbols of my existence. My products are training experiences. I also think of myself as a steward of the mind." For most Motivators, it's not enough to just work at what they love, they desire to create good and leave some visible evidence behind that they helped others. This visible evidence can be in the form of a change in another's life, something tangible that represents the Motivator to future generations or something that aids others, but the Motivator who created it is forgotten.

Another trainer said "I like being challenged. The cases where people don't think I can do it, I like to go in and prove that I can. It's a gotcha. For example, when people don't expect to learn because I'm a woman. I like to create an environment that will initiate growth. I love to see their attitudes change." Her ability to overcome great odds help this Motivator to move into new directions.

These Motivators seem to also learn by giving knowledge to others. They like to help people to understand. One commented, "I really like making things clear to people."

Some admit that they like to lecture because they "like to ham it up." Within these types of Motivators, communicating the message is as much fun as seeing the results. In someways it's probably similar to knowing a secret and then sharing it with someone. Being the first to tell someone information can be exciting. Part of the thrill seems to come from watching the expressions on the faces.

Their mission is to communicate and help others grow and mature. To do so, they have the opportunity to learn the information first. These Motivators can be classified as devoted learners. Being naturally curious, they make excellent researchers. They use their observations of nature and personal experiences in their messages, much to the delight of their audiences.

This group of Motivators plays a crucial role in producing significant changes in people's lives. Their brief encounters serve as catalysts to new ways of thinking, new directions and new behaviors. Many people claim it's a privilege to be their audiences.

SALES PROFESSIONALS

The Motivators who serve as sales professionals usually motivate and influence out of a desire to help others and make money at the same time. They are terrific at their profession because like the previous group, they are professional communicators. Similarly, they like to feel they are helping people.   They also know that in the long run if they don't serve their clients well, they won't have clients.

These Motivators enjoy the thrill of the market place. They enjoy creating desire for their products and services. "The charge I get out of it," was the response by one professional when we asked him why he was in the profession. They also enjoy their company perks. One Motivator commented that "it wasn't that I set out to go into sales...the company was attractive and there were little ego type pluses. Doing a traditionally male job was an ego trip."

These Motivators seem to love the challenge of selling. If you have ever tried to sell anything, you know what a challenge it is. These Motivators are stimulated to keep pushing ahead.   They work long hours and push themselves to produce more. We observed they are truly achievers and will continually go after higher goals unless someone or some thing redirects their paths.

THE HELPING PROFESSIONALS: THERAPISTS, COUNSELORS, MINISTERS

This unique brand of Motivator helps people to meet their psychological, spiritual and career needs and goals. They typically chose their profession because of personal circumstances or personal needs to help others.

One pastor, Dr. Harold Ellens explained how growing up during the depression helped him to decide to become to be a minister and therapist, "The net result was that my whole childhood seemed to me to be under a rather awesome cloud of generalized suffering and anxiety among everybody that I knew in the community. The only real experience of significance, transcendence and resilience was the experience of life in the church....So I remember that very early I made a rather aggressive decision that if there were any way that I could figure out how to do it, I was going to undertake to change the circumstances that had brought all those people into that kind of painful experience."

One Motivator described herself as a Christian Worker, who "enjoys working with people and developing their commitment to spiritual values." She and her husband help potential missionaries to prepare for overseas' cultural shock. She is an analytical Motivator, who is able to help people get to the root causes of spiritual and psychological pain. The Motivators in this category truly care for the people they serve.   They sincerely wish to help others grow and develop to their full potential.

The therapists and counselors have become skilled analyzers of human behavior and attitudes. They are able to care and empathize with their clientele, yet remain professionally distant. Their missions are often ones of healing and creating growth. Fascinatingly, they are able to give and heal without draining their supply of motivation. Most communicated that their work enriched their own lives and that they thrived upon the energy of their client sessions.

HEALTH CARE PROFESSIONALS

The professional Motivators are a special group of givers. Although some found themselves in the profession because of outside influences, they typically chose their work for altruistic motives. They like to give and help others feel better. They often use their medical knowledge and intuitive knowledge to effectively serve others.

One professional stated..."I needed to have a job that was substantial and I needed to be able to support my children following my divorce. I needed to have a stable career for myself and I needed also to be able to feel that I had a purpose and I could serve a community and could serve people as well."

Motivators in the health care professions commonly put others' needs before their own. Through giving, they motivate others to good health. Their missions give support to all of us from time to time when we most need it and are most vulnerable. They like to see people get well because of their efforts.

MANAGERS, SUPERVISORS AND LEADERS

This special group of Motivators seldom receive the praise they deserve for their work of holding everything together. Their work is typically one to one although they may also motivate and influence groups. Most find their work challenging. They are responsible for keeping the nuts and bolts of the organization together.

These Motivators see themselves as individuals, who have a special role to play between upper management and their workers. The most effective ones seem to communicate a "we're in this together attitude" to their workers. Knowing their people's needs and desires, they are able to respond appropriately.

Some feel they could make more money in another profession, but they like the responsibilities and challenges of their work. They enjoy working with others to accomplish organizational goals and objectives.

One manager perceived herself as a "professional communicator" because of the nature of her work. She went on to explain..."everything I do entails taking concepts and synthesizing, integrating and explaining them to people for different reasons, sometimes for their understanding, sometimes for persuasion, sometimes just to keep a process moving. I spend a lot of time working with people, communicating and making sure that things happen. I manage and I do a lot of different things but I really think of myself as communicating with people."

Research has indicated in the past that managers and supervisors spend about 80% of their time communicating. A great portion of that time is probably dedicated to the process of motivating to obtain results. For the Motivator, motivating and communicating are interwoven expertly into the fabric of managing of people.

OTHER PROFESSIONS/OCCUPATIONS

Certainly, being a Motivator is not limited to these occupational areas. You can be a Motivator in any occupation. These were the ones we chose to study in depth.

THE MOTIVATORS' EARLY MOTIVATORS: ROLE MODELS

We have mentioned that many Motivators knew what they wanted to be very early in life, while others "through fate" seemed to fall into it. Undoubtedly, these choices were inspired to some extent by the Motivators' Motivators or their role models. In many cases the role model influenced the Motivator's character strengths and sometimes their choice of profession.

The underlying role model commonalties include communication, inspiration, encouragement, loving, caring, lively, humorous and determined. Some of these people subtly influenced each Motivator to believe they could become and do terrific things. Others unconsciously provided examples of behavior and were personally attractive to the young Motivator. They often had unusual personalities and were able to show their strengths.

Having one historical and several family role models, Margaret Bucklin, Home Economist, described them to us, "my paternal grandfather was a very active person...certainly a very hard working person...he was a leader in the community and could do many different things....very serious and didn't relax enough. My maternal grandfather was always easy going. Both were successful but very different.

My one grandmother was somewhat of a leader and very efficient. The other grandmother was creative in how she would get things done, also easy going."

She continued, "I also think of Eleanor Roosevelt, because of her leadership and how she spoke out ... not because she was a very attractive person but all the things she was accomplishing...I certainly admired her."

One enterprising sales executive described his early Motivators as "your super heroes, Superman, Robinhood, John Wayne, and Henry Fonda. I also read about people that made it from rags to riches, those types of success stories to get an idea of how they did it."

Another Motivator described what was common for numerous Motivators, "I had a couple of teachers, who knew how to really develop people through positive role modeling."

As a child, this Motivator, who is currently an executive, described his role model as "a man who lived down the street from us...he and his wife sold clothing...he was a salesman...a very sincere guy. I used to polish his car and I used to think it was my obligation to keep that car in top shape and he wouldn't let anyone else touch his car. He was a great inspiration to me after my father died about what's right and what's wrong. He also believed if a kid does a good job let him know it and stay on the positive side."

The Motivator's Motivator played a significant role in the formation of the ideals, character and direction for each of these Motivators. Some provided balance in personality traits. Others provided a standard of behavior to emulate. Still others gave the Motivator the ability to be confident and have a healthy sense of self esteem.

SUMMARY

As you can see you can be in almost any occupation and be a Motivator. Whatever your occupation, it can be a vehicle for delivering motivational energy to others.

A-4
DISCOVER
YOUR
MOTIVATOR
STYLE

Throughout our research, we found many different ways to motivate and various styles of Motivators. Although no two people are exactly alike, they sometimes have similarities. The Motivators we interviewed and have met, usually have a predominant style but are very capable of using several other styles. The receiver of the motivation can also provide the need for a particular style or styles to be selected.

Motivators can either be true or psuedo in their motives and methods. The Motivator's style can be truly motivational or it can be a psuedo manifestation that lasts only a short period. Most Motivators we interviewed indicated the motives behind the motivation differentiated between the true from the psuedo Motivator. In this chapter the styles can be viewed either as true or psuedo, however we discuss them from a truly motivational perspective. There are two groups of Motivator styles: the Movers and the Shapers.

THE MOVERS

The Movers are a grouping of Motivator styles. Movers charge ahead with clear direction, perseverance and speed. Frequently they use dramatic approaches. Being highly charged, they exude a tremendous amount of energy. When you're with them, it's quite obvious that they are Motivators. You easily recognize this quality in them the first time you meet them. You feel the force and impact of their personalities as they present their motivational messages. They seem to have a way of emotionally charging you.

When we interviewed these styles, most of them immediately recognized they were Motivators after hearing the definition. The styles included in the Movers are the Racers, Exhorters and the Negative Pygmalions.

RACERS

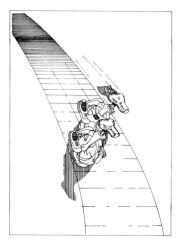

This Motivator races through life, constantly doing things. The Racer is usually an extrovert who might be described as a bit showy. Constantly doing more things than most bodies can handle, the Racer is continuing to think of more. Living life at an accelerated pace, the Racer is always or almost always out there hitting the deck running and usually doesn't give himself or herself any breaks. He or she doesn't want to allow the body to recharge, therefore is very susceptible to the Work Addiction Cycle we discuss in a later chapter.

Some Racers can go on like this for years. They are always on mentally. They like to be off and running on a new project and dragging everyone else with them. They resemble a drill sergeant who puts the troop through their paces. Only they are the troop and the sergeant all rolled up into one.

They like and are motivated by challenge and variety. They challenge themselves and others. Their goals drive them to perform up to high standards. They willingly sacrifice other parts of their lives to reach particularly challenging goals or to accomplish their missions.

As alert and active individuals, they have a hard time slowing down and are likely to keel over at the end of a day. They have a hard time turning off their minds because they are multiphasic in their actions. It's quite natural to find them working on multiple tasks or projects at the same time and frequently working long hours. Being ambitious, they like to push themselves to their outer limits of endurance and seem to have a gigantic capacity to do so. This can relate to the number of hours worked or how much they accomplished in a day.

They're highly energized thus accomplishing exceptionally difficult or huge goals. They give off an enthusiastic energy and are fun to be with because you get caught up their dreams and ideals. They like to be around people. They quickly create emotion and excitement within others.

They will push and drive themselves until physical exhaustion overtakes them. They are also susceptible to the work addiction patterns we discuss in the second section of the book. Often they lack having a balanced life with recreation in it. Their health and families suffer because of their goals or missions. They do a lot of good for others. Unfortunately, those closest to them suffer from lack of attention. The greater need of many creates the sacrifice for the few.

Racers have a strong sense of time urgency to accomplish as much as possible in limited amounts of time. They lack the patience with others who do not move as fast as they do or don't get as excited as they do about things. They like living life in the fast lane and don't hesitate to change lanes without signaling if they think of a more workable idea. They need to see results more quickly than the other styles. New developments must be constantly occurring from their efforts with people. They'll willing put in a year or two but they are not as likely to go an extended period without the encouragement of steady and visible progress. For longer projects, they frequently divide the major goal into subgoals with corresponding daily objectives to achieve. They have a strong need to accomplish visible results and need to see their milestones and markers along the road. They reward themselves for achieving their milestones. The reward typically comes from inside regardless of what others tell them.

They easily influence and work with others one to one or in groups. They use gestures and words to motivate others. They often lead by their verbal statements of motivation. They are the ones who go beyond feeling you can do it, they tell you can do it and believe in you. They use many group enabling statements and behaviors such as "we'll beat them" or "we're the greatest team." They make you feel a part of a special team. While they use challenges to motivate themselves, they use nearly impossible challenges for others, too, through the use of quick deadlines and high quotas. Then they are very likely to use "we can do it" statements to get the group moving. They have learned to lead by using these challenges and team approaches to accomplish the impossible mission.

A good example of this behavior was given to us by an executive we interviewed. He described his early managerial experiences in a small Asian country managing a company. "It was really very backward, no growth and not a profit environment. I think it can be described as a loser. We set about to do some things with the people. In this culture, people don't cooperate if they don't agree. We decided we'd have a sales contest for the first four months of the year and we also had one against the three other subsidiaries in the region which were very good. I felt if we could really get the people motivated and somehow win that contest, we could start a whole new attitude process and show the people we could be winners. Then we could set different standards to continue to challenge ourselves. Then we would never fall back. Well, we got pretty lucky. We won that contest and we won it hands down.

We just blew the three subsidiaries out of the water. We did it by getting everyone in the company involved. Communicating with everybody, holding meetings...it wasn't a big company about 100 people but we'd hold meetings every two weeks, then once a week and when we got down to the wire, we met every day. The whole idea was to get 100% involvement and everybody thinking about doing the same thing. We were just a small sales company. The only person we had to serve was the customer, not ourselves. The people really got behind it.

The really interesting thing was when it was all over. All these people were gathered in a service bay and I told them that they came in second and that I was really really proud of them and that never before had the company had that kind of growth. They didn't believe me and everybody was kind of solemn. Nobody said anything and I said 'what's wrong?' and I said you should be absolutely elated. Finally somebody in the back of the room said 'we don't believe you.' I said 'what do you mean by that?' He said 'we think we won!' I said 'Yah, we did!' The whole place went nuts. As a result we doubled then tripled profits in three years. Later we did things, nobody dreamed could be done with the same people." Racers such as this know explicitly how to capture the support of their people.

EXHORTER

They are performers before groups of people. They typically have excellent public speaking talents. Frequently, they appeal to the intellect of those they motivate.

To turn his or her motivation on, the Exhorter typically whips up a personal excitement level for the moment of being on stage. However, the moment, he or she leaves the "performance" stage, another kind of personality switches on. Indeed, you might not believe he or she was the same person you saw on stage or in the training session.

Some religious leaders seem to fit into this style. "He/she gets up there on the pulpit and is gun-ho raising his/her level of motivational pitch and raising the audience to same extent as well. A moment after the message, he/she has changed the pitch."

Prior to going on the Exhorter psyches himself or herself up like an athlete getting ready to go on. The Exhorter might express it thusly..."This is a part of my job, a part of the role." At the extreme, the Exhorter will deliberately to get into that super frenzied state of motivation in the preparatory stage.

Sometimes, the Exhorter transforms from a bud to a beautiful blossom because of the mission. He or she easily changes from a quiet personality to take on the role of the personna to become this larger than life personality. The Exhorter enters this stage as a different person. On the motivational stage, he/she is truly inspiring.

Some Exhorters work with a single person while others work with groups. Sales people usually work one on one and occasionally with a whole group. When a sales person becomes a manager, one of the major problems he/she faces is motivating a total group. It's a different type of skill and purpose than when selling to one person. His/her talent may not be in motivating groups as much as it is in motivating one person. One to one, a Motivator can communicate monumental ideas. With a group, the Motivator needs to sense the levels of the participants regarding understanding, interest and enthusiasm, and vocabulary. A mass Motivator as an Exhorter uses the intellect and intuition to judge all these factors and adjust for the group. The single Motivator may be thinking and judging the individual's needs of the moment. The one to one or single Motivator can't focus on the total group but they can with one, two or three. Most Motivators have either ability and may have difficulty switching to the other style.

The mass Motivator described it thusly: "in front of a group, I turn on a theatrical side of myself because I know I need to be enthusiastic, lively, humorous. As the group gets to know me, then I communicate in a more intimate way. People need to trust and like us before we can communicate at a greater depth."

The exigence has created the need for this Motivator to be this other person. It happens when the Motivator walks up to the front of the group. The group personality turns on in the Motivator. Even when a specific question is asked, the mass Motivator integrates the information and relates it back to the total group's needs. Part of it may be fear of the group of strangers. The Motivator wants the message to be accepted and so the role is taken on in order to be personally accepted.

Their personal motivation again relates to a mission. Quite often they are willing to fight for the good of many. Typically, they have large missions reaching expansive numbers of people. The other manner in which they motivate is to persuade others about a larger issue.

Their sense of urgency is not as strong as the Racers, the intensity of compulsion is missing. They seem to have a belief that what ever their cause, it will be carried on after their life time or without their immediate presence. They enjoy initiating but they seem to know the work will go on even without them. They plant seeds for generations.

Their rewards come in the form of group adulation and the realization of their power to inspire others to reach higher levels of goals. The thrill of seeing others responding in excited and enthusiastic manners is an energy source which they feed upon. These dynamic reactions sustain them.

Also, they tend to be humanitarian and altruistic in their choice of missions. They inspire and exhort others. They are able to ennoble those who come to hear them speak. When they are finished, their audience has become ensnared in a much larger cause than when they first arrived. Commonly, they are the preservers and expressers of the values and higher laws of a culture.

The potentially negative quality that we see with these people is their lack of follow up strategies. However, others like Billy Graham, have taken steps to formally set up groups who will follow through with people after the Exhorter has moved on. Others leave and have not planned for a means of sustaining the enthusiasm they create. Without some follow up structure, recidivism can easily occur for those they exhort.

There are at least two types of Exhorters: those who exhort others to do something for mankind and those who exhort people on a personal basis to do something great for self. So it can either be some grand mission relating to humanism or a simple version of "light your candle in your own little corner of the world." Some of the more famous ones are probably Wayne Dyer, Leo Buscalia and W. Clement Stone, who publicly exhort people to become all that they can become.

They typically have a singular message to communicate to large groups. Some might have become Exhorters through a metamorphosis from the Spiritual Motivator or Responder. This naturally happened as the mission became larger than a one to one focus.

They convey a sense that they are speaking to you individually even though you're in the middle of a large group. Leo Buscalia does this exceptionally well with his message of love.

NEGATIVE PYGMALION

He or she motivates negatively in a similar fashion to the sergeant in the movie "An Officer & A Gentleman." He constantly told the protagonist "You can't make it, you can't do it." This motivated the guy to even stronger efforts. Remember the intense scene where he was doing push ups. The sergeant tried to convince him to wash out. At the end, the sergeant was the person, he had the most respect for. The sergeant pushed him through the hard course and kept him focused on the target.

One of the Motivators described her experience with a teacher who was a Negative Pygmalion. "This teacher who pushed me, in a way forced me into change and growth. Later, I realized that she helped me and motivated me more than a positive Motivator would have at the time. I really needed it. It created a mental toughness. You see, when you're already good there's a tendency to be mediocre. She pushed me to be better. She wouldn't even consider letting me stay at my level but strove to push me forward."

Negative Pygmalions serve a particular role if the appropriate exigence is there. You are forced to find the motivation within yourself. It is probably a time when you need that extra push. It can be done at a conscious or unconscious level.

The positive Motivator says "Oh you can do it," which doesn't have the same effect because you are thinking of dropping out and you can't do it. A Negative Pygmalion makes you angry enough to prove your worth to yourself. You're motivated not because of but inspite of. You find the driving force within yourself.

Some of them know by acting this way that they'll get this response. Their

motives are good. They know this is the spur that will get the person going.
Usually they have great insight into human behavior and know which tool
even though it's a negative one, will trigger this person into action and
develop their potential. They are a rare breed of Motivator. They are unlike
those who use negativity to destroy--they are using it constructively. Their
mission is to make the person do more or to realize full potential.

Coaches and teachers are prone to do it. Sales people, who won't let people
buy their product, play the role of "you can't have it." They play skillfully by
using their knowledge of human behavior. Managers will use this if they
believe a person's ultimate good is to push people to their peak performance if
all else fails. This motivator is skillful and knows not to take the person to the
breaking point or hurt the spirit. You crave to prove them wrong. These
people know you have more good in you and their job is to bring you to that
level.

This style of motivation is most effective with and should be limited to people
who are lazy, have given up, are afraid of moving because they fear failure or
those who just seem to be wallowing in their own glory and are stuck. Those
who need this type of motivation are motivated more than they would be by
Exhorters or any other style of Motivator.

THE SHAPERS

These Motivators move forward in a less
dramatic style than the Movers. Shapers are
much more quiet and relaxed in their
approach to motivation.

By quietly shaping behavior through
listening and responding to individual
needs, they motivate in a very subtle
manner.

They had more difficulty recognizing that
they were Motivators. It was only through
reflection and looking back that they were
able to say "Yes, I guess I am."
Shapers include Responders, Secret
Motivators, Balancers, the Spiritual
Motivators and the Analyticals.

RESPONDER

They like to bring out other's potential but they don't see themselves as Motivators. They respond to needs because they are givers and willing to share all that they can. They can be self sacrificing and taken advantage of by others. Some people will take up too much of their time talking to them but Responders see the person's needs before their own. They care about others. They often want to spare others pain because they themselves have experienced the pain.

They are more likely to use their analytical skills than to use strong arm techniques. Their motivational methods are usually through their actions and limited amount of words of encouragement. Others seek their advice and counsel when they are in trouble. They will take the brunt of the anger, knowing once the anger is spent the child or person will be able to logically deal with the problem. They are able to take a lot of abuse because they are strong and know they can take it. They have a lasting effect on people. They are very supportive to keep the person going. They influence by buffering the impact of the problem by encouraging the person to step out, keep moving or charge ahead. They quietly tell the person to keep going. All they want to be is a part of the process, they don't demand to always be there. Often they launch people or help them release themselves from being stuck on a sand bar but they seldom see the person finish.

Perhaps this is the secret behind the Horatio Algier story, too. The Responder motivates because he or she starts so far behind the rest of the population.

Another perspective comes from the hare and tortoise story. Having a seemingly tortoise personality of shyness, miraculously, he or she blossoms into the motivator based upon personal experiences and ability to translate those experiences for others. The translation skill brings forth the motivational ability to the surface.

There is no apparent sense of urgency regarding their missions. This Motivator can work for an extended period without the encouragement of progress because they recognize that people may need more time to achieve the Motivator's hopes and aspirations for them. They will wait for progress. They have a strong belief in the ability of people to succeed over the long haul. They are responding to others needs thus they position themselves to help but not to seek those who need help. Their scope of motivation is limited to those who recognize their strengths and seek them out. They can get easily walked on but they don't perceive it in that manner although their families and spouses are protective of them. In a strange manner, they are like sacrificial lambs.

By quietly motivating others by behavior and actions, the Responder accomplishes more than by using words. People feel better about themselves having been with this Motivator. A quiet strength is translated to others. Many parents and some coaches fit this role. Coach Tom Landry is a Responder who consistently exhibits gentlemanly behavior. Some religious leaders are probably operating from this category. You're more likely to hear or read about how they motivate by example.

This Motivator is passive and more relaxed than some of the other styles. When she or he is away from the work situation, the ability to cut the intensity off turns on.

They react to the exigence. They don't plan to motivate but they do it. A need is there and they will respond to that need. Parents, teachers and coaches often follow this Motivator style. Some children can convey the strength of this style to their parents through their expressed comments and their actions. Often in single parent relationships this occurs rather than the mate bonding. The child articulates to the parent the belief that Mom or Dad can pull through a difficult time or that the parent has certain qualities or character strengths that will take charge and overcome the difficulties. The parent may not have the certainty of faith that the child has. The child seems to be able to see a strength that the parent is unaware of.

The movie the "Champ" reveals this Motivator style used by a child to influence the father to enable him to realize his potential.

Probably, Red Skelton is another example of the Responder. During interviews he is a very quiet gentle person. He becomes a totally different person when he's playing San Fernando Red in a skit. He puts on the mask. It's not a false mask but the need to accomplish the mission requires the clothing of himself in the personae.

Typically, you learn more from reading about them than by being in direct contact with them.

SECRET MOTIVATOR

This is a tough one to find to interview. The Secret Motivator is a kind of Responder who does motivate but doesn't tell anyone. We know they exist as subtle workers, who may not even be aware that they influence. Sometimes the recipient doesn't know the Motivator did it.

THE BALANCER

As a hard worker, this Motivator puts boundaries or limits on life while focusing his/her energy. Balance is the order of the day, which is reflected in a social life, family life, and having a productive work life. The raison d'etre (ie.,reason to be) is to enjoy all those segments of life, work very hard, inspire others and motivate others. Although giving is an important aspect, one segment is not allowed to totally to take over this person's life like the Marine Motivator does. The intensity of the energy is very high but controlled. These Motivators work very hard in what ever role they're in but when it's time to switch to a new role, they switch. If he sees someone who needs a pep talk, it's given. If she notices someone needs a challenge, it's created for the person. The motivation is intentionally focused and regulated. This person has things under control in his or her personal life by structuring time and activities. By closing doors or limiting their time to a few people, these Motivators know what their limits are and do not like to be pushed beyond them. This focused position is communicated in a quiet yet resolved manner. They are like a laser beam with a very narrow focus but it's also very strong.

For example, the kind sympathetic supervisor at work would not be the same if you called him or her at home. In order to work with them others must be able to pace themselves with the Balancer's structure and limits of time. They perceive others impinging upon their time so they will cut your time short if you don't move quickly enough for their time frame. A sense of impatience is communicated to others they help if the person hasn't done anything with the advice. Their sphere of influence is limited because of their self set boundaries. The degree of influence and amount of people influenced is far less than some of the other Motivators.

The Balancer's sense of urgency is also focused and limited but it is not all consuming such as the Racer. The energy of the urgency is placed upon "I must be doing versus I must be accomplishing." The white rabbit in Alice In Wonderland states "I'm late for a very important date." Their focus is narrowed in on the activity at hand rather than on the achievement of the goal.

Their pacing allows them to survive over the long haul. Rarely do they burn out but if they do it's a slow process. They are the least likely to be a work addict. They are probably not as spontaneous because of their structure. The Balancer cares and is concerned about others. She or he plans and does survive for the long haul. For example a missionary wants to save a person's soul no matter how long it takes. Instant gratification isn't always available and isn't a goal. Sometimes it may take years to see a return on the investment.

An advantage of this style is "when she is with you, you feel the intensity of this thinking and acting person but if you're not the focus of her laser beam you can easily sense your time with her is limited." The structure that this style sets up to enable him or her to achieve can also act as a barrier. One Balancer mentioned that when people call her at home, they will get a totally different response than if they had called her at work because she is in a different role. At home she considers that time her personal life and will not respond as well as she would at work.

Their focus is singular...one project or task at a time. They tend to do more private motivation than in public groups.

This hard working Motivator usually gives complete attention to the segment currently being focused upon. In addition, he or she still has something reserved for self. Playing the role of Motivator at work is known as one of many roles. Key Statement: "This is my job to be motivational but I don't have to be that if I'm on my own time." He or she works hard on motivating others and self on a consistent basis. One person interviewed works long hours and he knows he should give to his family so he trys to adjust for his family for awhile. Then his work calls for more of his time. He responds to the need at the time. He's humorous, somewhat laid back but can get really excited by something new.

SPIRITUAL MOTIVATOR

In a mystical sense, the Spiritual Motivator is sent into individuals' lives when they most need this motivational element. They operate on a higher plane of conscious that is not understood by others. They have a recognized talent that is brought in to help others.

One example was described by a Motivator, who wrote an article and gave the rough draft to another Motivator who in turn gave this draft to another person to read because she needed it. The writer was shocked that they liked it because it wasn't a finished product and even more surprised that it was of spiritual help to this third unknown person. The writer's intent was to express thoughts and perhaps help others but surely not prior to the article's publication. She hadn't even placed her byline on it. The Spiritual Motivator inspires people in unexplicable ways with seemingly no intent.

Another example is one of the interviews for this book with Dr. Harold Ellens. Even though we had intended to make this a positive focusing book, Dr. Ellens inspired one of us to new conclusions and spiritually heightened awareness about the reason for the positive focus. Prior to that we were committed to the focus on an intellectual and factual basis without full intuitive commitment.

Spiritual Motivators are seemingly sent into people's lives, often in the strangest ways and places. Perhaps there is a higher level of consciousness going on even though the Spiritual Motivator is unconsciously aware of it. A higher cause seems to motivate them. They seem to be guided into making certain contacts and responding to others' needs. They like to initiate or enhance growth or development. This is a key element of their missions. They are very likely to use positive words to help others such as "You can do it" or "I believe in you." They see potential in someone and will comment to that person about it in order to inspire the person. One such Motivator made a comment "I believe that you're going to do great things. You have a great potential." to another woman during her senior year in school. This style of Motivator has a tremendous intuitive power and can effectively inspire others for a life time. They are discovers of the individuals who are diamonds in the rough. They are able to detect the special potential in others. They have an aura which radiates caring and love for others. They are highly motivated to deal with the intangible aspects of life to improve themselves and others as they seek to reach their full potential.

Their sense of urgency can be stated "I only have so much time (this life time) to accomplish my mission." They have a solid commitment to spend their time wisely and in a concentrated manner. Generally, they will sustain their efforts and will not give up. Their greatest weakness is they have a limited store of energy and if it isn't replenished and often it can't be, they will become exhausted. Unlike the Racers who have tremendous energy supplies to drive their motivational efforts, the Spiritual Motivator expends more energy. The essence of their energy is psychologically and spiritually intangible. The intensity of the effort by the Spiritual can easily drain them. This style mostly gives out and it's not as easy to restore Spiritual energy as physical energy. They enjoy what they are doing, however, once the energy is released to someone, it is seldom returned to them so that energy is gone. This creates the sense of urgency to give a lot before their resources are depleted.

They recognize their sacrifice is needed to fulfill a greater cause. The giving up of their individuality is to achieve a greater good. If they choose to give too much, it can be a destructive force for them personally.

At times others become too dependent upon the Spiritual Motivator. These dependent people can very easily drain the Spiritual Motivator without using the energy for positive change. Mature Spiritual Motivators are aware of the possibility of being depleted or realize it's happening and ward off the dependent person. The Spiritual Motivator has to say "No, I can't meet with you that often" or "I can't talk now (on the phone) I have many things to get done." They must halt the requests from the dependent person before it damages their energy source. They need to realize that equal amounts of energy refilling them must be receive for the amounts expended. Otherwise they will experience a downward spiraling cycle of lower and lower energy available to give out.

Their focus is plural and public to help many. They can exhort one person or many. As you can see, they appeal to the spirit or the soul of those they influence. People love to be around Spiritual Motivators. Their personal self esteem is improved by the comments made by these Motivators. Having an uncanny ability to see deeply into a person's soul, they massage the part that needs loving by sensing and giving what the person needs. To do this though, they essentially drain themselves of energy. Thus, they need to take frequent breaks from the intensity of giving to recharge. Most need supportive people to give to them and protect them from others.

One Spiritual Motivator commented that she has to hear the pain of a problem expressed by someone at least twice before responding. "I ask questions to determine if they really want me to inspire them. I have given out far too many pearls to swine in the past only to have the hogs eat them up without using them. I refuse to do it because it hurts me inside. I have learned a person has to be ready for the message, maybe that's why I have to hear the pain 2 or 3 times before I respond to it."

THE ANALYTICAL

The Analytical uses problem solving techniques such as the Socratic method to help a person solve a problem rather than telling the person to figure it out by himself/herself. The Analytical Motivator can use this internally as well as externally with others. They frequently will answer a question with a question such as "Well, what do you think?" or "How do you feel?" They have excellent interviewing and communication skills and will use this style more than giving direct advice to others. They are skillful at reading between the lines and the body language of others. They motivate others by asking challenging questions and can use the Negative Pygmalion Style to help a person. They constantly draw conclusions from all aspects of life and challenge others with these thoughts. They are very intelligent people who love to think and translate their intellectual thoughts to others.

Potential for intellectual growth challenges them. By asking questions that require thinking, they serve their missions of helping others. They don't want to be given the answers. They like to search and enjoy discovering the answers for themselves. Having a strong desire to solve problems, they tend to complete what they start. Their concentrated strength of seriousness is interrupted by their ability to laugh at the world. This sense of humor provides chuckles to those around them.

Possessing an extended sense of urgency, they are able to seek the answers at a leisurely pace. Some don't believe they will find the answers in their life time so they don't feel the need to be the one to find "the" answer. A piece of the puzzle is enough to satisfy them. They enjoy "the moment" more than the other styles. As historians of facts and conclusions, they like to inform others about these. For them, the process is as equally important as the end product.

They are stimulating to be around yet can easily wear others out with their thinking capacity to stretch the mind. Some require more time than others wish they would use. They tend to be very deliberate in their thinking process, which can drive others crazy.

In order to learn the answers, they are perseverant and willingly ask unpopular questions that they feel need to be asked. They like to help others to think at a higher level of intellectual pursuit. They enjoy learning whether it has an application or not.

Sometimes they forget to put other balancing parts of life into their activity schedule. If they are intrigued by a question, they will concentrate on uprooting the answers. Thus they neglect to take care of themselves.

Occasionally, their conversational methods are irritating when they ask the who, what, when and where questions and their respondents don't wish to give it. This kind of curiosity can be very annoying.

They are at their best at one to one or in small groups.

SUMMARY

What ever style of Motivator you are, you have much to give. You can use different styles with different individuals or in different parts of your life. Most Motivators have one or two predominant styles, which are used frequently.

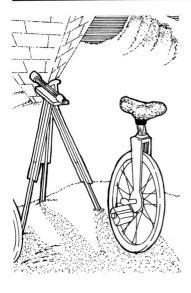

A-5
WHAT ARE THE MOTIVATOR'S VALUES, PASSIONS, SECRETS AND COMPULSIONS?

From the very beginning of our exploration, we knew the Motivator personna was complex. Our analysis of the complexities has yielded a wealth of insight. We have uncovered some of the secrets about the Motivator phenomenon such as their values, passionate and compulsive drives, and their feelings about projects and peak performances.

Motivators are activated by their values and beliefs, their work and other people. Perhaps this isn't very different from the rest of the population but their internal motivation creates something wonderful in others. By being, by speaking, by directing, by encouraging, by acting, they motivate others. This is no slight achievement, when so many people wish they had such ability.

AMONG THEIR VALUES...

Motivators like to be in control of work and life around them. They value independence and autonomy. They have a strong sense of where they are going and the direction others should head too.

They prize creativity and tend to be very creative themselves; sometimes the creative result of their efforts arrives in a wholly new form and rhythm of working with people. One Motivator stated..."The creativity of ideas can create a driven orientation for me. Work can become the ultimate mistress seducing me to want to do more because it feels so good."

An idea can captivate them. When this happens, they seem to relax their standards regarding time and its use. For example, the authors admit that in the beginning stages of conceiving this book, we willing met with the original project team during some off times such as Sunday mornings. We were each excited by the prospect of accomplishing the book's mission. The benefits always outweighed the consequences in those early stages.

Other values include self sacrifice and giving. Unfortunately, Motivators sometimes willingly sacrifice to the point of being sacrificial lambs.

Perseverance and persistence are also highly held values, which Motivators expect of themselves. A problem occurs when Motivators don't know when to stop. They can be like a dog gripping a bone...they keep going until they achieve the goal, drop from exhaustion or learn another way to handle their energy and dedication.

An educator described this need quite well. "This pattern was established by the seventeenth century Russian social scientist, Zigarnik, who determined that we are beings who must complete our work. If we leave something unfinished, our minds will continue to work on it. Motivators don't like unfinished business...they will drive themselves to complete a task. Unfortunately, working to help people, the work is never fully finished."

Healthy Motivators have learned to let go when people, tasks, things or situations are no longer rewarding. They will even choose to ignore the need to complete the task. Likewise if a person can't be helped, Motivators limit the input they provide to this person and go on to help other people.

Motivators like both excellence and high quality in their work and the work of others. They strongly dislike mediocre performance. They are always striving to pull people one notch above their adaptation level. They want to see others stretch, grow and use their talents. Indeed, many have the ability to stimulate such people to new heights of achievement and belief in their abilities.

Others are encouraged to strive for excellence, not perfection. They know people have these abilities and they expect them to use them. Their belief is mediocre behavior and work is unacceptable. One Motivator alluded to a Biblical parable of the landlord which exemplifies this principle. Prior to going on a journey, a landlord gives money to 3 servants. Two of the servants each doubled their money. The third servant buries it. The landlord rewards the first two generously. The other one is condemned for not even putting the money in the bank.

When a person is perceived by a Motivator as not fully using his/her talents, the Motivator will attempt to activate him or her positively and often, this input makes the difference in that person's life. He or she is no longer satisfied to live less than at his or her full potential. This value provides not only the person with more to live for but also benefits others.

Motivators are truly pleased with other's hard work. They love to hear of success stories of those who have worked hard and gain success through their efforts.

SELF MOTIVATED

Motivators are full of energy and ideas. Their drive has earned them the respect of their peers. Perferring to move forward with their ideas, they challenge themselves to gain new growth and accomplishments. After many years of being self starters and igniters of others, this self motivated behavior is thoroughly embedded in their grain.

One interesting comment came from a highly motivated sales person, who described what she does when she's undermotivated: "I kick myself up the back side. You can not be up all the time, but I only allow myself the luxury of being down for short periods of time and I say that is a luxury because it really is a luxury to wallow for a little while, feeling sorry for yourself. But I never allow myself to do that for any length of time. I suppose the reason it's so easy to get out of it is because if you look around there are so many other people who have worse problems or so many more problems. I mean it's really kind of ridiculous and an ego trip to keep yourself down and in that hole for too long."

She continued by saying "Now if I get up and I'm feeling that I need to be motivated, I remind myself that I'm not doing this for me. I'm doing it for God and I ask for strength to go and do the best job that I'm capable of doing that particular day. It's one day at a time and I just trust that it's going to happen and realize that I'm not doing it for myself. I'm doing it for the other people that depend on me, I'm doing it because God wants me to do it or I wouldn't be here and because I really don't want to let myself down either."

Another person described the process of becoming motivated by saying: "there's some sort of spark. Something just happens. I just get an idea, there's a little flash, just like the light bulb thing. I usually get it about five or six o'clock in the morning. Sometimes it will be an idea that will keep me going for five years. There's something else going on underneath in my subconscious that keeps me going because I really can keep going. There have been a few people, but I think basically I motivate myself."

Beliefs in God or some higher power than themselves, belief in what they're doing and church experiences were mentioned as motivating influences by some of the Motivators we interviewed.

A middle manager told us..."The biggest way that I become motivated is to believe in what I'm doing. If I really believe in something, I'm highly motivated. I motivate myself."

Joan Tirak commented "I am primarily motivated by being alive. I am motivated by my faith in God, my faith in the goodness in humanity, my belief that everything works together for good if we work with it. I'm motivated by those who work in my work. I am motivated by love."

Still others spoke of synergy and the need to be a part of where the action is. Note Sandy Parker, a social worker's comments about how she becomes motivated: "I just think I have a real strong sense of curiosity about what's going on and a real need to be a part of things and participate in things and I think I also have a real strong need to be effective. My need to be effective and to be creative are real fine motivators for me."

Motivators turn their inner motivation into an energy release that creates powerful desires within others. Many Motivators have kept their child-like desire to consistently produce something new for themselves and others. For them, motivation is harnessed energy. They have learned the secret of turning the tremendous energy of enthusiasm into the motivation to create and produce. They are motivated to create this same enthusiasm in others. Just being around a Motivator can be exciting and yet somewhat hazardous because of the draining effect. Perhaps, it is because they are givers and consumers of energy, simultaneously. People are drawn to some Motivators because of their enthusiasm and vitality. Their racing thoughts often test their companions' endurance and abilities to absorb stimulating conversation.

THE MOTIVATORS' WORK ETHIC

Motivators have a strong internal sense of direction and purpose. This deep sense of purpose is exhibited by their determination, perseverance and acts of caring and giving to others. In addition to placing a high value on the achievement of their missions, they value hard work.

Most grew up with a derivative of the protestant work ethic of working hard in order to be worthy of heaven. A good example of this influence was expressed by Joan Tirak: "my family were industrious and perfectionists. We had a humble home, a simple home, we had everything we needed. I learned that if I wanted more I had to work for it. For example, if I didn't want hand me downs, I had to learn to sew and was sewing my own clothes in 5th grade."

A close facsimile of the protestant work ethic was identified by this Motivator's belief..."I learned that when you worked hard and did a good job, you pleased people and therefore were looked upon as a good person and a nice person and so you had value. If I pleased other people, I was OK."

Another derivative shows the loss of the reasons for hard work, but placed emphasis on the act..."I think I've always believed in hard work. The ethic in the home was just work, work, even on the weekends." stated fast paced sales manager.

Still others learned that working hard was a fact of life to be accepted. Note the comments by these two Motivators:

"There's a saying about my family that nothing comes easy for us, we always have to work for what you get. So my parents worked very hard to have what they valued in life....I think I just accepted the value of work for work's sake that there's something intrinsically good about being able and doing work," commented Jan Urban-Lurain, a manager in a Michigan governmental office.

A competitive salesman told us his view of work and life..."Mainly I learned not to expect other people to pay your way and if you want something out of life you have to work for it, you can't expect other people to accomplish that for you."

Another derivative was the platitude..."Do the best you can." This one created problems for some who found they could always do better. One, in particular, remembers the impact of the 4-H Motto: To Make the Best Better. "For many years, it created a sense of striving within me. I could do my best but when I had done that, I could always do better. Until I realized in adulthood that I was worthy, not based upon my achievements but upon who I am, I had been continually chasing one goal after another. First I learned to reward myself after achieving a goal, then I learned to say 'you're OK just the way you are,' and later I learned to accept my fears, mistakes and just enjoy the moment."

Doing your best had positive effects as well. Another Motivator told us what her mother had said to encouraged her, "Do the very, very best job you could possibly do. No matter what you do. Put your best forward. I didn't have the work ethic that people have that you work for a dollar. I had the work ethic that you work for self satisfaction and a good job done. It's personal and with that would come recognition...whatever you wanted."

A variation on the need to do "the best you can" is the need to perfect. For some, being and doing the best is enough. Others are never satisfied with their own work. They believe it can always be improved.

Ernest Hemingway is said to have rewritten The Old Man and The Sea over 40 times. One Motivator recalled this statement's impact on her during college: "I remember thinking if I rewrote a paper only 6 or 7 times it couldn't be good because I hadn't done as much as Hemingway or as much as I was capable of. I never stopped to consider that maybe that standard was applicable for Hemingway and his book but for some very valid reasons it was not suitable for my writing.

There can be hundreds of possible reasons Hemingway rewrote the book over 40 times. Perhaps...

* he enjoyed writing and saying it in different ways,
* it required it because he wrote poorly,
* he was a perfectionist,
* each day he wrote, he saw it from a new perspective,
* he didn't want to stop writing because then it was done. Being done can mean you have to prove yourself all over again. This can be frightening."

PASSION FOR HARD WORK

Motivators thoroughly know the meaning of working hard and diligently. Others often note about a particular Motivator: "he works hard or she really puts her mind to it." Working hard for the Motivator means will power, discipline and single mindedness. Full effort is often given without a consideration of giving less. Motivators seem to love to give their all. Motivators work hard for a variety of reasons. Many expressed a sense of satisfaction and pride of working. Others admitted it was to overcome feelings of low self esteem. Achievement lures many Motivators to work hard.

"Hard work brings satisfaction because you choose what satisfies you and you give it all you got. It brings a sense of fulfillment, gratification and satisfies your hunger to do something to make your life worthwhile." Satisfaction is the motivating force for this Motivator and others. Many expressed an underlying need for fulfillment. Hard work easily fills this void because its results are so very visible.

Most view work as a wonderful experience. They receive many rewards from working. In some ways, the act of working provides a supercharged energy and sense of excitement. Some may even succeed in hiding this emotion from others, but most will say they enjoy their work. Indeed, they enjoy it far more than this statement implies as can be observed by the intensity with which they work or by their willingness to work on numerous projects simultaneously.

Working gives them a mental high.   When working, they can be extremely happy, loving every minute of the activity. They are creating. They are causing things to happen. They are in control of their destinies as much as they can be. No one tells them to work. They are always beginning a new project, thinking of a new idea or developing a new product or service. Motivators prefer multidimensional work to one dimensional activities. Most work on numerous projects and activities in a day's time.

From their perspective, life is work and work is love.   This attitude separates the Motivator from the rest of the population. Frequently, they find their missions encompassing other aspects of their lives.

Some Motivators stated they felt good doing hard work. Working hard creates motion and movement toward something either mentally or physically. Forward movement is always perceived in positive terms. There is a sense of accomplishment even as they begin to tackle the new goal. Some see the end as they begin and don't perceive the work in between as difficult. Others greet the work as an opportunity to show themselves what they can do. A salesman aptly described these feelings: "I can't see it as hard work. Sometimes I say 'yea, maybe I'm overdoing it a little bit,' but that's where I feel most comfortable, when I know I'm over the limit, have overextended myself. That's when I feel the most satisfaction. I'm 110% plus, not 100%. It's like I'm getting more out of the product than one expects you should. I need to do it! I want to do it! It gives me satisfaction and rewards me in my own way. Not so much financially but it just fills a need that I need to say 'hey I accomplished it, I did it. I overcame an obstacle!' It's like an obstacle course, you're running in a field, and I see the goal and I go for it. That's why I do it."

For many Motivators, the tremendous thrill of discovering their limits accompanies the satisfaction of proving themselves to themselves.

Obstacles become challenges to be worked through. These challenges must be present in order to feel a rich sense of enjoyment. Internal or intrinsic needs to work hard also play an important part in this scenario. The analogy "no gain without pain" applies to their view of work. If success comes too easily, the satisfaction may be less.

Typically, Motivators do not take the easy road of expecting less than their best. Many find hard work the way to express their value to the world.

Susan Garrity, an executive in a high tech company described her motivation for hard work thusly: "I am an achiever and I know there are no limits to an achiever. I believe given any task I can do it if I have the stick-to-it-iveness, tenacity and mental attitude that's necessary to keep going on, despite all odds. It's not unlike being a competitor in the Olympics. It's a fact that you're racing with the world and you believe you can do it."

Motivators are very seldom inactive. Inactivity demotivates them unless it's perceived as relaxation or rest. For some, it's a more of a deep seated problem linked to their self esteem. They believe if they are idle they are lazy. In these Motivators' minds, "lazy people" are worthless. Therefore, if they are lazy, they have no value. Being lazy for them can include an "off" day, not working on the weekend, relaxing after a hard day, and even vacationing.

What these Motivators fail to recognize is the fallacy of working to feel OK. We all need to mentally rest for at least a short period of time. The healthy Motivator knows that it's OK to take vacations and to relax at work along the way. Granted idleness can make some feel uncomfortable at first, granted. Ultimately though, it can make them more productive because their batteries have been recharged.

One individual commented about this phenomenon: "When we're not working, we feel we are not being productive and we don't like that feeling of having down time. There's a conflict. We have carried this to the extreme by being multiphasic. Multiphasic means that we are able to easily do two or more things at once. For example, even when we're not working, our minds are still going. Where ever we are or even we're suppose to be relaxing, we are always making larger interpretations from a simple circumstance and applying it to life."

The typical charged up Motivator works far more than 40 hours per week. Even if he/she is not working 16 hours per day, the thinking and analyzing continues through the waking hours.

The Motivator's work provides a major portion of the enjoyment they experience. It provides a focus for living. Several commented that work is life to them.

Some perceived hard work as a means to overcome a low level of self esteem. One woman commented that she used to work hard in order to establish her identity as a good person. Unfortunately, working hard only exacerbates the problem of self esteem. The vicious cycle of doing more so one can feel alright causes some Motivators to do more and receive less fulfillment. The need to have a healthy sense of being happy with yourself can't be filled by satisfying a need for recognition or a need to achieve goals. Self esteem originates from self acceptance rather than from other's acceptance or the visible results of hard work.

WHAT IS SUCCESS?

Given their perception of hard work as a strong positive aspect of their lives, the Motivators' views of success revealed a myriad of values. Some admitted they were not there yet, as if success was a place to be. Each had a clear picture of what success was for them. Most Motivators measured success from an intrinsic perspective such as self fulfillment, freedom, tranquility, serenity and growth, although some did define it as recognition and material benefits.

One individual saw success in terms of her behavior: "If I'm consistent with what I feel I could be as a person and faithful to those things that should be priorities in my life, then I guess that's the thing that I measure and that becomes success or failure. It's not a real external thing for me, it's more internal."

A mentally healthy view of success was given by a therapist...."My definition of success is feeling good about you and what you do. If you feel good about it and enjoy what you're doing that's success, you've made it."

Jackie Lichty, a sales executive with the 3M Company explained "It means serenity now. The people that I seem to gravitate toward, are people who seem to have this inner calmness, a sort of peace of mind. They're not the strivers and the achievers that I used to admire and want to be like but I seem to be gravitating toward these other more passive things and those people have something that I want. I also recognize that the two aren't mutually exclusive."

Another fascinating view was expressed by a successful consultant, Marilyn Hubbard: "Success to me is being able to enjoy the simple things in life. Freedom is important to me...being able to do what I want to do is successful to me. I'm kind of a simple person and I like to do simple things but also if I want to do something extravagant I need the money and resources to do that. So I guess to always have the options and to always be able to exercise the options under my own control. Success to me would be being in control and responsible for my own destiny and having the resources that I need."

A long term perspective was provided by Dr. Harold Ellens: "I think for me success is growth. I feel very consciously that human life is designed as a process of moving along a continuum of growth from a very primitive state of development at birth to the total self-actualization and self-realization of all of the incredible potentials with which each is invested. I think that's what the image of God in us is, that wonderful array of potentials, and that life is the process of achieving fulfillment of all those."

An educator who perceived success from an accomplishment viewpoint told us: "Success means achieving something and feeling good about it. Success does not mean to me more money, more status, more opportunities to do things necessarily. It's a personalized sense of achievement. It feels good."

The values of hard work were expressed in this man's sentiments about seeking success: "Success means looking back at your own accomplishments, reflecting back, if you will, and having learned from what it took you to get there and not lose sight of the perspective of how you got there. Success means

to me having goals that are just an inch away from what your hand can reach
but not unrealistically cause then that's no goal. It has to be attainable.
Watch, you reach that and something else becomes another goal and you
keep reaching. That's success: one goal after another."

Setting goals is a very natural action for the Motivator. Healthy Motivators set
achievable goals in reasonable numbers. Motivators unaware of or refusing
to acknowledge their own limits may set unrealistic goals. They usually
become depressed when they are not able to achieve them.

EXPERIENCING PEAK PERFORMANCE

Motivators value being alive. Most seem to enjoy living life to its fullest
whether at work or elsewhere. When they talk about performing at their peak,
they glow with excitement and enthusiasm. As hard workers, they love to
experience the peak performance. They see themselves as organized,
perceptive and having a high energy level. With pride, they discussed their
ability to have several activities or projects going at once. In their responses
they clearly defined peak performance, to enjoy it and seem to seek it.

A sales manager talked about peak performance in terms of energy...."I have
a lot of energy...very high energy...I feel happy inside. I think that
enthusiasm comes forward and other people pick up on it....I am mentally
sharp and have heightened perception of what's going on around me and a
heightened ability to be able to put a lot of different things together to make
some kind of picture...tremendous sense of perseverance like no matter what
the road blocks, we're going to overcome those. Nothing is going to prevent
us from achieving the objective...tremendous sense of excitement."

Sandy Parker, a social worker commented about the healthiness of it: "Kind
of a zing..I wake up and I feel a lot of energy. I relate to people very deeply
without all the addictive behaviors involved. I think I express myself very
clearly. I feel a sense of fun...just a sense of joyfulness about being alive."

Ronna Hoffmann-Albers described her peak performance behavior as a
Training Director: "When I am at peak performance, I am organizing a crisis
so there's lots of stuff flowing in. I'm analyzing it, organizing it, setting out
what needs to be done with each piece.   Separating and sorting it into
categories and deciding which category has to come first and getting to work
on that category or getting someone else to work on it."

APPROACHING NEW PROJECTS

For many, the peak performance excitement emerges at the beginning of a
project. The excitement seems to be connected with optimism and the
anticipation of realizing the possibilities.

Others expressed some apprehension when starting a new project. They were
fearful of being overwhelmed by the immensity or the aspects of doing
something new. Most admitted they had to adjust their thinking so they could

begin in an optimistic frame of mind. Motivators are human, too. Their frailties come to the surface from time to time. Sometimes they fail but they seldom step back from trying.

THE SECRETS AND SURPRISES

Would you believe that Motivators are not always highly charged and stimulated? Some expressed that they too, need time for recharging their energy levels. They do experience down times, brief as these may be. A few of the Motivators we spoke to were actually a bit depressed at the time we interviewed them. Fortunately, they know how to get motivated again and seldom stay at the low ebb for long unless they are experiencing burn out.

Like everyone else, most Motivators like to be appreciated. They love being noticed and rewarded. They find this attention spurs them on to new heights.

Most Motivators indicated that they motivate themselves more than others motivate them. Realizing that if they are to achieve what they want to, they have to light their own fires. Waiting for others to inspire them can mean a long wait. Strange, isn't it, that what they can do for others so easily is so seldom done for them?

Surprisingly, while about a fourth of the Motivators mentioned they were stimulated by their own goals and objectives, only one specifically stated that the process of helping others motivated him.

Even Motivators can be self deceptive. In their heart of hearts, they may know a weakness but never admit consciously. Sometimes, they will be so busy that they don't analyze themselves. Sometimes, the mission is in control of them instead of their being in control of their mission.

IN SUMMARY

Motivators' values, passion for life and work and even their compulsions make them an unique and fascinating personna. Without their inner drives and desires to be, to achieve, and to motivate they would not be Motivators. In this chapter, we've tried to give you a sense of the heart beat of this personna. Each provides a tremendous service and benefit to those in his or her sphere of influence. Yet they are much more than the results of their presence upon the earth. They are people to be cherished and enjoyed because of who they are.

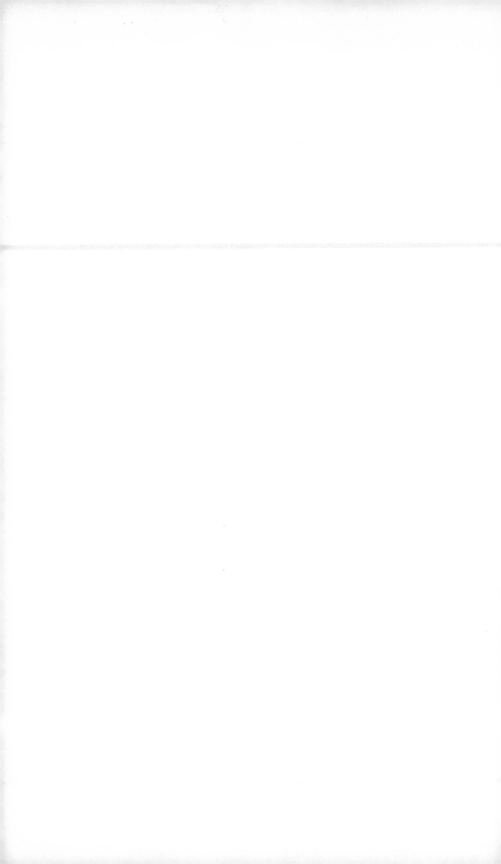

SECTION B:
THE POWER DRAIN

B-1
BEWARE
OF THE
MOTIVATOR'S
MIND LOCK

Life can be viewed as a paradox, a series of theses and antitheses . We accept these opposites: day and night, good versus evil, givers and takers, winter and summer, the Alpha and the Omega to name a few. Opposites can be observed everywhere.

This principle can be applied to the personality of the Motivator as well. While possessing great strengths, the Motivator also has the potential for equally great weaknesses, which can create personal havoc. For all the motivational and enthusiastic strength, this person exhibits in the work place, there is a very fragile skeleton of physical and psychological capacity.

It has been said that a weakness can become a strength. Similarly within a strength, can lie a great weakness with the potential to destroy the Motivator. The Motivator's mind lock is potentially capable of ensnaring the Motivator in a cycle of pain and strain.

WORK ADDICTION

The Work Addiction Cycle is the Motivator's mind lock. One can become a Work Addict without having any prior inclination to it. The Work Addict typically tries to balance his/her life between work, responsibilities and leisure time prior to entering the addictive cycle. Social interests are pursued until the work load becomes overwhelming. Occasionally she or he becomes involved with work to the extent that work is life and life is only work.

He or she usually enjoys and may even love his or her work. For some work addicts the thrill of working, controlling numerous activities and achieving gigantic goals excites and tantalizes them to commit more time than is physically, intellectually, emotionally or psychologically healthy. The Work Addict will pursue the work activities until the tasks are complete or he/she burns out.

UNDERSTANDING THE PHENOMENON

For Motivators involved in the Work Addiction Cycle, moderation is a four letter word. Some believe they can continue at their rapid pace forever. Many do have the capacity to do more than others. Work Addicts often enter this addictive cycle because of their desire for a "thrill," a need to fulfill their lives by helping others, or a personal work ethic firmly embedded into their value systems.

THE WORK ADDICTION CYCLE

Unhealthy Motivators either don't know their physical and emotional limits or they choose to push themselves to the brink of these limits. Desiring the "buzz" of handling more work, some will willingly walk down a narrow path to emotional and physical exhaustion. The unhealthy Motivator or the one who has a slight case of temporary insanity will enter a Work Addiction Cycle.

A series of behavioral stages emerges with slight variations for individual personalities. These stages can cover weeks or years. Some of the people we interviewed said they were at different stages depending on the projects they were involved with. The majority admitted they felt it was a fairly accurate description of their behavior. Numerous others said the first two or three stages were the most reflective of their behavior and they avoided stages four and five.

Let's examine this potentially problematic behavior pattern.

THE WORK ADDICTION CYCLE

STAGES	BEHAVIORS AND WORK AND ACTIVITIES	CHARACTERISTICS OF PHYSICAL & EMOTIONAL REACTIONS OR RESPONSES
1 START UP	Ambitious projects selected Work Begins Seemingly unlimited energy	Enthusiastic Excited about a new idea, High level of productivity High Adrenalin Level Strong sense of satisfaction Sex drive may diminish Some fear of failure possible

PERSONAL TRAITS

Sense of purpose or mission in life
Likes to think of and take on ambitious projects

**2
GEARING
UP**

Pressures mount
Agreeably accepts more work
Continues to think of new ideas
to implement
Less personal time is spent with
family and friends
More time is consumed by
working
Leisure activities are reduced

Physical energy waning
slightly
Start drinking coffee or
alcohol
Feel powerful
Sleep patterns change
Original dead lines are
perceived as
less reasonable in light of
additional work
Start to ignore
the body signals
Skip or delay meals
Feel and believe in
control of everything
Still enthusiastic
Enjoy sense of euphoria

PERSONAL TRAITS

Willingly relinquishes personal life/recreational
activities to do more work
Enjoys the power of controlling many goals/activities/tasks
Wants to be in the seat of power and control

YOU CHOOSE EITHER STAGE 3A OR 3B

**3A
OVER
DRIVE**

You regain perceptual
control of your life and
activities
You either cut back activities
that provide little direct
reward or you begin
to delegate
You release control of parts
of the project and believe
others can handle more
of the details
You finish the projects,
experience success and
reward yourself

Fear of failure/success is
no longer an issue
Experience
overwhelming sense of
relief
Show respect for health
through diet and exercise
Psychological attitude
improves, you know you
are a winner

PERSONAL TRAITS

You realize you no longer have dues to pay nor
have to prove yourself to yourself or others
You know you are a success and the completion of
the projects, activities or tasks is not the basis of your
self concept
You face the underlying fear of failure and stop
trying to be in total control

OR

3B IN HIGH GEAR	Work has become your life Still productive/Mentally Capable Bring work home or stays longer Begin to say "no" to more work Driving without left brain help	Becoming fatigued Physically breaking down Less enjoyment being experienced Feel guilty about not being able to handle every detail effectively or personally

PERSONAL TRAITS

You wish you could do more
Compulsion-Commitment to others drives you
You want to handle more but feel you're losing
control over what you have

IF STAGE 3B IS CHOSEN INSTEAD OF 3A, THEN THE NEXT STEP IS STAGE 4

4 DOWN SHIFTING	Afraid of failure/success Afraid of incompetence Increased pressures from deadlines,clients, or self imposed values May only sleep and eat when not working Afraid of being an imposter: "If they only knew the real me." Perceive little or no feedback on performance Put important matters on hold	Drained Compulsion pushes you forward Tired most of the time Mentally wearing down Accident prone Drinking more coffee to make it through the day Don't acknowledge pain May reach breaking point Afraid people think you are incompetent but you are afraid to ask Snapping at others

PERSONAL TRAITS

Compulsion pushes movement
Belief: "Commitments must be fulfilled" drives your work
Don't want more work
Tell yourself to hold on a little longer
Low self esteem
Feeling out of control

CAN CHOOSE STAGE 5A OR 5B

5A SLIPPING THE CLUTCH	Illness, physical exhaustion or burning out prevents you from finishing	Physically and Mentally exhausted
	Someone else either finishes the work or it is left uncompleted	Feel like a failure and may wallow in self pity or ask others for pity
	Typical comments: "I worked really hard but no one appreciates the effort" or "I'm the only one who works hard, knows what they're doing and cares about the work."	

PERSONAL TRAITS

Use others, illness, and the difficulty of the work as
an excuse for not finishing
Experience fear of failure, so take the easy and somewhat
respectable way out
No self esteem, seeking pity and made himself/herself a victim

OR

5B GEARED DOWN	Reach the finish line	Physically and Mentally exhausted
	Everything is completed	Illness easily occurs
	Still in work gear, experience difficulty shifting gears	Not sure of level of success
		Can easily become involved in arguments

PERSONAL TRAITS

Need to rest but can't
Becomes nervous resting
Post Work Syndrome-Regret it's all over
Sensitive to other's comments about almost anything

These five stages with their branches represent the Work Addiction Cycle. Some Motivators experience this in different intensities. Some do not experience all of the aspects of every stage.

A healthy Motivator starts projects, gears up, shifts into over drive while flourishing physically and mentally. Most projects have a natural manner of flowing from start to finish in Stages 1, 2, and 3A. The healthy Motivator by using the preventive and avoidance techniques in the next chapter doesn't proceed through the negative aspects of Stages 3B through 5A or 5B. Although the project continues, the healthy Motivator has developed a new way of perceiving the work load and doesn't feel overwhelmed or out of control. Stage 3A can allow the healthy Motivator to start projects with enthusiasm, gain control versus being controlled and finish as a winner while evaluating mistakes.

Stages 3B-5 represent the danger points that can lead to a downward spiraling process of a person becoming an unhealthy Motivator. The unhealthy Motivator unknowingly traps himself or herself in the latter stages of the Work Addiction Cycle.

STAGE 1: START UP

Stage 1, START UP begins with the start of one or two new projects or new job. You find yourself excited with the creative juices flowing as you commence. You may be launching a highly ambitious project. (Most Motivators love to think of or accept ambitious projects.) The results of your work will probably be visible to many people.

We noted earlier that most Motivators have a proclivity to live life at an accelerated pace. Usually, the Motivator has more ideas and desires than any one person could handle in a limited time period. In fact, the Motivator personality is a ready candidate for high stress or even burnout because he or she is so highly motivated and desires to be in control of many tasks or activities.

In Stage 1, you accept the project because it plays a significant role in your purpose or mission in life. You may even perceive that your previous experiences and all of your skills have prepared you for just such a project and that this project was created for you.

Strangely, some Motivators experience twinges of the fear of failure just before they begin the project. Perhaps it's because of the project's visibility. The questions that come to mind are..

"What if I can't do it?"
"Is it possible. I could fail?"
"What will others say if I don't succeed?"

An executive noted. "I acknowledge it and when I acknowledge it, I overcome it. In the past, I haven't acknowledged it and it immobilized me. Usually I'm very fearful and intimidated by whether or not I'm up to it. After I dispel all that and say first step starts now, it's OK."

As the work begins, you find it extremely satisfying. You are very productive. This productivity spurs you on to a sense of euphoria. You experience a sense of living up to your self expectations.

You have a bountiful supply of energy. You even may believe that the supply is unlimited. You could work all night if you wanted to, right?

Stage 1 is called the Start Up stage because you have an over abundance of enthusiasm. This stage resembles a rocket taking off from a launch pad. It's full steam ahead and straight up with excitement and energy.

Planning and initial implementation are the types of work activity that occur steadily during Stage 1. When most of the planning is done, you begin the actual project or activity and work extremely hard. You achieve a certain amount of success, which brings more work from other sources or the original source or you think of more tangents to follow.

STAGE 2: GEARING UP

When the pressures start to mount, you've entered Stage 2, GEARING UP. In this stage, the rocket begins to turn ever so gently with its own trajectory. The path becomes curved, however, because the pressures of additional new ideas or new work are added.

The underlying desire is "Oh goodie, more work." In this stage, you are reaping the benefits of a very productive Stage 1. You're also continuing to think of new ideas or activities because you're probably exhilarated by the positive comments you're receiving regarding your new ideas and ambition. Positive reinforcement seems to spur you on to new developments.

Originally, the deadlines seemed to be reasonably set. Then more work comes your way. Can you handle it? Sure you can. This stage continues with more work and less time to play. The Gearing Up Stage may continue for months or years. The people who suffer in this phase are your family and close friends because they are seeing less and less of you. Typically, they begin to gently nag or so it seems to you. After all, you're enjoying yourself in achieving more and more.

If the nagging works you try to schedule time for them. This may even work effectively until you find you've slipped into the poorer of your choices...Stage 3 B, IN HIGH GEAR. There is a choice...Stage 3A, Over Drive, which provides a way out of the Work Addiction Cycle. The first time through the Work Addiction Cycle, most will be succumb the power drawing them in Stage 3B.

STAGE 3B: HIGH GEAR

When you have arrived at Stage 3B, In High Gear, you're putting in long hours. In fact, you're spending less and less time outside of work. Every moment outside of work you're either thinking of it or wishing you were doing it. Yet if you are an unhealthy Motivator, you're becoming very tired. You have begun to feel guilty about not doing more. You've made commitments and you wish you hadn't. A paradox occurs, your mind is saying you should do more and your body is saying I can't take much more.

Fatigue begins to set in and you start to ask yourself, in one form or another, "who motivates the Motivator?" It's not why am I doing this, but can I continue to hold this pace? You push yourself to the outer limit of your physical strength because you've made a commitment to someone or to yourself. This sense of commitment continues to drive you forward day after day. And it drives and drives. You may even feel guilty for not doing more in less time. Why, you ask yourself, are you questioning your ability and energy to complete the work?

After all, you're the Motivator, the person with the solutions, not the questions. Others look to you for help, guidance, encouragement, information, inspiration, advice, and excellent work. They expect it from you. Whether you're a manager, teacher, counselor, doctor, salesperson or in some other helping profession, you give and give. People expect you to continue giving. You probably gain a lot from your giving, much more than money. You love to work and produce.

Yet, there comes a point when the work itself is not enough. It's no longer fulfilling, it's become a burden to bear.

You've become worn, perhaps physically exhausted. You're ready for retreads, only they don't make them in people size. So you just continue in the downward spiral of physical exhaustion.

One Motivator described it thusly, "As someone who helps, trains, inspires occasionally and motivates others, there comes a point where I can no longer push effectively."

STAGE 4: DOWN SHIFTING

Stage 4, DOWN SHIFTING arrives when you begin to fear failing or begin to wonder if others think you're incompetent. This is a critical stage to even the most mentally healthy person. How you answer it will affect your ability to cope with the rest of your life.

You're probably noticing that you feel tired all of the time. You can't seem to catch up on your sleep even if you do take a weekend off.

In this stage, your compulsion clicks into gear. You only sleep and eat for brief periods of time. Those are the only pleasures you allow yourself. One Motivator described how she avoided looking at the clock just prior to retiring at night. She would set the alarm for the necessary wake up time but refused to calculate the amount of sleep she would obtain each night for fear the small number of hours would burden her mind and thus reduce her achievements. This worked for awhile until her physical being started to show the strain and her friends and family began to comment.

Another Motivator told us of how she would argue with her Doctor about whether she should rest today or next week while experiencing a raging fever. She had so much to do, she found herself negotiating with others and herself inspite of overwhelming knowledge that she needed to rest.

Another noticeable physical symptom is smoking more or drinking more coffee during the day. Motivators in this stage will do anything to keep themselves moving forward. The stress created from the pressures seems almost overwhelming.

Some of the Motivators experienced the fear of being an imposter, thinking "if they only knew the real me, then..."

Regretfully, no one is giving the Motivator feedback on the performance or the Motivator is not asking for feedback. This deeply hinders the motivation. The Motivator continues because of compulsion and personal pride but may feel rejected. You may even be afraid that you are incompetent but you don't want to ask because they may agree or begin to think so because you asked.

One unique aspect of this stage is that the Motivator no longer expresses the desire to do more. The strategy now is to hold on just a little while longer. He or she voices to the self "You can do it. Keep going and it'll soon be over."

All important matters other than work are put on hold until there's time to adequately deal with them. Here the Motivator acknowledges what should have been acknowledged in Stage 2, that he or she can't do it all.

A few Motivators experience the difficult trap of fear of success. Those who fear success realize they can achieve it but fear the pressures success will bring in order to continue to live up to their own and other's expectations of them.

STAGE 5A: SLIPPING THE CLUTCH

If you enter Stage 5A, you are essentially SLIPPING THE CLUTCH. You can no longer stand the strain, illness, physical exhaustion or burn out has control of your life. You are afraid of finishing the project because it won't be perfect or it may even mean you have to admit failure. So your subconscious takes over and you become sick. Deep down you feel like a failure and your only recourse (or so it seems) is to quit before everyone else discovers it too. There are many excuses that you can use to receive pity and support from others. You can't enjoy success so you enjoy self pity because you don't want to admit failure, the fear of failure or the fear of success. The work is left undone or someone else must complete it. You may ask others for pity by saying such statements as "I worked really hard but no one appreciates the effort" or "I'm the only one who works hard, knows what they're doing and cares about the work the way I do."

Unfortunately those who assume this position experience a lowered sense of self esteem because their rationalizations are never enough to support a truly higher sense of self esteem. They are playing the role of the victim, yet being a victim is not necessary if they could face their fears. By not facing it, they continually face the same experiences again and again.

STAGE 5B: GEARED DOWN

Stage 5B, GEARED DOWN represents the opposite but equally negative finish of the Work Addiction Cycle. You complete the big project or many projects and are about to begin the next set. You may take a vacation or you may not. If you do take a vacation, the odds are you will want to be back working. Most likely, it won't be enough to break the Cycle. If you don't take the vacation or rest at work, you will either repeat stages 3B and 4 or you're headed for physical exhaustion and/or burnout. You need to analyze your perceptions of the work loads, fears, need to control and your level of self acceptance.

Several Motivators, we interviewed mentioned a branching effect occurring for them or the addition of a sixth stage. One person described Stage 3A as the transition between Stage 4 and Stage 5, which integrates the elements of both stages. She saw as a part of the syndrome that "I kept climbing the mountain, and there were always mountains to climb, and I would climb one mountain after another and I never gave myself a chance to sit at the top and enjoy the view, because the minute I got up there, I didn't see any peace and serenity, all I saw were more mountains to climb."

Another person described Stage 3A as an alternative to the last three stages "you realize you're going to be a success and you draw strengths from that and you'd realize that you're in control and you don't have to deal with all this stuff. That you will take control of your life and whatever project you're involved in, you will be successful and so it doesn't matter. You may have to work a lot of hours but the body has never died for lack of sleep. So you don't have to worry about that so much. It's mainly mental in any kind of endeavor." This Motivator has been able to overcome the mental weariness by drawing strength from this sense of control. He has the spiritual, physical and psychological ability to overcome the Work Addiction Cycle and to leave Stage 2 or 3B to move to Stage 3A. He is also suggesting a different perception of dealing with working on projects or activities.

Many Motivators who experience this cycle don't recognize their negative responses until they have reached Stage 5A or 5B and are exhausted. Some continue to experience the negative responses because of lack of recognition of ambitious work desires. One Motivator aptly described the phenomenon: "The road to excess leads to the castle of wisdom. How do you know you've gone too far? If you haven't seen the castle yet you haven't gone far enough." If you have reached stage 4 or 5, you are probably scrubbing the walls in the castle of wisdom. You have definitely gone too far.

We will further discuss the alternative route of Stages 1, 2 and 3A in the next few chapters. Briefly, it allows you to avoid the negative responses of the Work Addiction Cycle.

IDENTIFYING WHERE YOU ARE IN THE CYCLE

This quiz can help you determine if you fit the Work Addiction Cycle and at what stage you have progressed to.

SELF ANALYSIS
QUIZ

1. **ARE YOU EXCITED ABOUT A NEW PROJECT, THAT YOU ARE ABOUT TO BEGIN?**

2. **DO YOU FIND YOUR ADRENALIN LEVEL IS HIGH AS YOU START WORKING ON A PROJECT?**
   IS THAT TRUE OF YOUR WORK RIGHT NOW?

3. **ARE YOU CURRENTLY FUNCTIONING AT A HIGH PRODUCTIVITY LEVEL?**

4. **IF YOU ARE BEGINNING A NEW PROJECT, HAVE YOU HAD SOME FEAR OF FAILING?**

5. **ARE YOU AT A STAGE WHERE YOU HAVE FILLED YOUR WORK LIFE WITH MANY PROJECTS?**

6. **ARE YOU EAGERLY ACCEPTING MORE WORK BECAUSE YOU WOULDN'T WANT TO MISS AN EXCITING OPPORTUNITY?**

7. **ARE YOU BEGINNING TO SPEND LESS TIME WITH FAMILY AND FRIENDS?**

8. **HAVE YOU RECENTLY HAD TO REDUCE YOUR LEISURE ACTIVITIES?**

9. **DO YOU FEEL YOU CAN DO MORE WORK IF YOU JUST PUSH YOURSELF A LITTLE MORE?**

10. **HAVE YOU JUST BEGUN TO REALIZE YOUR DEADLINES ARE NOT AS REASONABLE AS YOU ORIGINALLY THOUGHT?**

11. **HAS WORK BECOME YOUR LIFE?**

12. **ARE YOU STARTING TO FEEL FATIGUED?**

13. **DO YOU WISH YOU COULD DO MORE, BUT YOU KNOW YOU PROBABLY HAVE TOO MUCH TO DO ALREADY?**

14. DO YOU FEEL COMPELLED TO FINISH WHAT YOU HAVE STARTED?

15. ARE YOU FEELING GUILTY BECAUSE YOU CAN'T DO MORE?

16. HAVE YOU BEGUN TO SAY "NO" TO REQUESTS THAT YOU DO MORE?

17. ARE YOU TIRED ALL THE TIME?

18. WHEN YOU'RE NOT WORKING, DO YOU ONLY HAVE TIME TO SLEEP AND EAT?

19. DO YOU HAVE SECRET FEARS THAT OTHERS MIGHT THINK THAT YOU'RE INCOMPETENT?

20. ARE YOU DRINKING MORE COFFEE OR SMOKING MORE TO JUST MAKE IT THROUGH THE DAY?

21. HAVE YOU RECENTLY SAID TO YOURSELF "JUST HOLD ON A LITTLE LONGER"

22. HAS ANYONE GIVEN YOU ANY FEEDBACK ON YOUR PERFORMANCE?

23. ARE YOU PUTTING IMPORTANT MATTERS ON HOLD?

24. ARE YOU ANGRY WITH YOURSELF OR OTHERS?

25. HAVE YOU EXPERIENCED AN ACCIDENT RECENTLY?

26. HAVE YOU RECENTLY FINISHED A PROJECT IN AN EXHAUSTED STATE?

27. DO YOU FIND IT DIFFICULT TO RELAX?

28. DO YOU NEED TO REST BUT CAN'T?

29. HAVE YOU EXPERIENCED A PHYSICAL ILLNESS?

30. HAVE YOU CUT BACK ON THE NONESSENTIAL TASKS OR HAVE YOU BEGUN TO DELEGATE MORE SO THAT YOU NO LONGER FEEL OVERWHELMED?

31. HAVE YOU FINISHED THE PROJECTS, FELT SUCCESSFUL AND REWARDED YOURSELF?

32. ARE YOU ABLE TO STRETCH YOUR PERCEPTUAL LIMITS TO HANDLE MORE WORK WITH EASE THAN YOU MIGHT HAVE THOUGHT POSSIBLE IN THE PAST?

33. DO YOU FEEL IN CONTROL OF YOUR LIFE AND WORK EVEN THOUGH YOU ARE WORKING ON MANY TASKS AND ACTIVITIES CONCURRENTLY?

34. HAVE YOU RECENTLY EXPERIENCED AN ILLNESS THAT PREVENTED YOU FROM FINISHING A HIGH PRIORITY GOAL OR OBJECTIVE?

35. DO YOU FEEL LIKE A VICTIM OF YOUR CIRCUMSTANCES BECAUSE YOU'RE ONE OF THE FEW PEOPLE WHO REALLY WORKS HARD?

If you said yes to questions 1-4, you are experiencing Stage 1. If you said yes to question 5, you moving from Stage 1 to Stage 2. A yes answer to questions 6, 7, and 10 are a part of experiencing Stage 2. If you said yes to questions 8 and 9, you are traveling through Stages 2 & 3B. An affirmative answer to questions 11, 12, 13, 15, 16, 17, 18 put you solidly in Stage 3B. Question 14 relates to Stages 3B through 5B, so a yes here means you are deep within the cycle. A no to question 22 and a yes to questions 19, 20, 21, 23, and 24 mean you're probably in Stage 4. A yes to question 25 and 29, may mean you're somewhere between Stages 3B and 5A or 5B. A yes to questions 26, 27, and 28 typically relate to being in Stage 5B. A yes to questions 30-33 indicate that you are probably in Stage 3A. If you answered yes to 34 and 35, you may be in Stage 5A.

Which stage are you currently experiencing?

You can avoid the negative responses to the Work Addiction Cycle with realization, self analysis and action to change your behaviors. We'll discuss these in the next few chapters.

B-2
WHY ARE YOU SPINNING YOUR WHEELS?

Why would perfectly "sane" people allow themselves to experience the Work Addiction Cycle? Are Motivators really masochists?

Perhaps. It all depends upon your point of view. The reasons vary from Motivator to Motivator. In this chapter we isolate the surface symptoms that can easily be seen by all but are not to be confused with the bedrock causes. The truly compelling issues lie far below the surface. To determine which apply to you, we suggest a time of soul searching and intense analysis of your motives. Some of you may find this examination uncomfortable. However we hope you will examine each of the surface and embedded reasons because every Motivator who has experienced the vast majority of the Work Addiction Cycle needs to learn how to move through and maintain the positive side of the Cycle found in stages 1, 2, and 3A.

THE WAND OR THE DAGGER

The Motivator holds a wand in one hand and a double edge dagger in the other. The major decision is to create magic with the wand or to destroy the Motivator and/or others by using the dagger. As described by our Editor, Jan Urban-Lurain, "The Motivator has the power to create or destroy. The wand represents the Motivator's magical talent to create, motivate and improve others and himself or herself. The dagger represents the Motivator's power to destroy herself/himself or others by willingly experiencing Stages 3B-5 of the Work Addiction Cycle in order to enjoy the thrill and excitement of it. It can also be an exhilarating experience to use the wand for positive reasons." The wand is exercising the choice of consistently experiencing Stages 1, 2 and 3A.

This choice is often shrouded in the love of working hard. Motivators sometimes unconsciously have a strong desire to use the self-destructive dagger. It can be disguised as the wand, the useful tool which gives the Motivator the power of control. While relishing work, the Motivator tries to satisfy an unquenchable hunger of becoming better and doing more. Power lures and then devours its Motivator victim in the later stages of the Work Addiction Cycle. Only when trapped in these stages does the Motivator realize the wand has been exchanged for a dagger.

The wand in the other hand creates magic. The Motivator uses the wand throughout his or her work. In fact, the wand produces many magical effects in Stages 1-3A. Waving it, the Motivator has a mystical power to influence and control other's behavior. Frequently, people are amazed at how much the Motivator can produce in a very short period of time. The amount of work whether it's the number of products sold, the amount of accounts sold, projects accomplished, or programs completed seems humanly impossible. Yet the wand has worked its magic because the Motivator is in control of his or her life in these stages.

The Motivator experiencing the last stages of the Work Addiction Cycle has traded the wand for a dagger. Typically he or she is working at full capacity (as close to 24 hours/day as humanly possible) for as long as it takes to complete the work. At this point, completing the task becomes the primary thrust not the sense of accomplishment. They may even realize their mental capacity is less than 50%, yet they push on. They are using the dagger to commit psychological and physical suicide. The choice of using the wand or the dagger is held by the Motivator and is based usually upon the knowledge or lack of knowledge about his or her true motives. After realizing these, the Motivator can more clearly make the decisions needed to avoid using the dagger.

COMPELLED BY AMBITION OR NEED FOR ACCEPTANCE

As we've discussed, Motivators are driven by the values connected to the Work Ethic. They are typically ambitious initiators, thinkers, opportunists, hard workers and willing to take on the world if the missions require such effort.

The pressure of the Motivators' value systems push them forward to achieve more. By achieving, they feel a sense of fulfillment and begin to accept themselves for what they do. By working hard, they hope to prove to themselves that they are really worthy of positive self esteem. These value systems are developed through the pain of experience. Some even pride themselves in how they are constantly striving to improve their inner qualities. They change and get better every year. They may even believe the cliche, "no pain, no gain." By getting "better" they become more acceptable to themselves and others, so they think.

Such value systems can easily trap these Motivators into traveling from Stages 3B to Stage 5 of the Work Addiction Cycle. This is the extreme culmination of their value systems when rolled to the farthest edge of their physical, emotional, spiritual and intellectual limits. Instead of feeling successful, the Cycle provides them with feelings of incompetence and failure. Motivators may think (like we did in the early writing stages) that it's the ambition, the work ethic and the thrill of work that creates the Work Addict. Yet when you attempt to solve the problem of the Work Addiction Cycle by reducing your work load, you can easily reenter the Cycle and experience this lack of satisfaction. The real answer lies much closer to the need to accept yourself for who you are and not for what you can do rather than blaming yourself for being ambitious. It's easy to confuse the need for achievement with the need to be accepted. At the very hub of the Work Ethic's motivations is the desire to be found acceptable. Work is perceived to be the way to become acceptable to yourself and others. Unfortunately this is or can be a misleading direction to choose.

BY THE SHEER STRENGTH OF THEIR WILL

Ella Wheeler Wilcox wrote in her poem "Will"

"There is no chance, no destiny, no fate, can circumvent or hinder or control the firm resolve of a determined soul.

Gifts count for nothing; will alone is great; all things give way before it, soon or late.

What obstacle can stay the mighty force of the sea-seeking river in its course, or cause the ascending orb of day to wait?

Why, even Death stands still, and waits an hour sometimes for such a will."

Will power can be a healthy motivational force, it can drive Motivators to accomplish Stages 1-3A. In its extreme form, it can compel them to continue through Stages 3B-5.

When they encounter Stages 3B through 5 of the Work Addiction Cycle, they believe they must dig in deeper and work harder. They will not give in. Many times they won't even admit their tiredness. They will joke about it, but keep going. They become robots and march ahead with their goals. Unfortunately, some Motivators forget that even robots need a source of energy. While they may even expect that others need to recharge, frequently they don't acknowledge this need in themselves. One Motivator described her feelings about completing a low priority task. "I'm my own worst critic and when I'm tired, I never give in. Not unless physically I can't do anything. New Years Eve was a case like that. My body was saying 'Look idiot we're through, you may not be mentally, but we're through.' I couldn't give in. Even in those conditions, I was still at the terminal working at 30% efficiency but still saying I'm going to win. At 11:45 p.m., I was getting some notices out to some clients wishing them Happy New Years."

In this example, the Motivator kept going until the strength was gone. It didn't matter that the task was inconsequential. What mattered was that she had set this goal for herself and she was determined to finish it.

Why do some Motivators choose to glorify the "will" at the expense of their health? Perhaps for some Motivators, it provides a way to show the world that they can handle almost anything. They need to prove to themselves and to others that they can be strong. This is a delusion.

When we asked Pam Czuj, Executive Director of the Personal Dynamics Center, her opinion about this phenomenon, she said "The overwhelming desire to drive oneself becomes more important than the task at hand. The goal becomes the medium and the medium becomes the goal. Unfortunately, the act of enduring in itself will not create real satisfaction because of the by products of Stages 3B-5."

As we pointed out earlier in our discussion of those stages, there's a self destructive element at work in Stages 3B-5 when the Motivator experiences complete physical and emotional exhaustion. This masochistic approach to work ultimately takes its toll.

AN OPPORTUNITY THAT YOU CAN'T REFUSE

Another significant reason Motivators unconsciously entrap themselves in the later stages of the Cycle, is the desire for the challenge and potential rewards of a golden opportunity. Someone presents an opportunity or they perceive an opportunity that is too good to resist. Even though they know it's too large for them to handle by themselves, they want it. The desire to control or to exercise power over work and people plays a pertinent part in the reasoning scheme. The pleasure of being in charge of a large project or to achieve an overwhelming goal can lead the Motivator to try to do more than he or she is capable of physically or perceives he/she can effectively do.

Greed, also, can lead to the Work Addiction Cycle because it's exhilarating to see how much you're able to do. In addition it's often too good to pass up. Someone else might get to enjoy the work. These create a desire for more. At this point, greed for power of controlling the various aspects of your life and work has firmly set in. None of us likes to admit we desire power over things and people but most will agree it's fun to be in control. Yet for unhealthy Motivators, the power to control found in Stage 2 makes them feel somewhat superior and provides a false sense of worthiness and self esteem. The more they control the more they need to control. This leads them into Stages 3B through 5.

This is the point where they can choose to be a healthy or unhealthy Motivators by deciding between Stage 3A and Stages 3B-5. Whether it's positive or negative depends on the Motivator's true capacity and perception of this capacity. Greed, the need to control and the desire for power, can destroy the Motivator as the intellectual, spiritual and physical capabilities become depleted. The Motivators who choose to ignore these negative responses go on to repeat Stages 3B-5 continually. They are totally unaware of their motivations for continuing. They are doomed to repeat the Cycle until they die, have a major illness or realize they have a choice between Stages 3A and 3B.

COMPULSION IS DRIVEN BY PERCEPTION

Some Motivators gradually become involved in the Cycle and build up momentum. They accept more work without even considering whether they can handle it effectively or not. They subconsciously have set themselves up for the negative responses of Stages 3B-5.

Once the Motivators reach this point, the centrifical forces seem to be too great to allow them to stop without hurting themselves or disengaging their values. Most would say they wish to escape Stages 3B-5 but their level of commitment won't allow them to do so. At a deeper psychological level, they are experiencing perceptual problems. They don't want to be responsible for having made the choice and its resulting Stages 3B-5 negative responses. They either deny that a choice existed or don't recognize it.

For those who have the negative experiences, they feel compelled because they see no alternatives. In Stages 1 and 2, having the inkling that they have a serious choice to make, they can bring it back into control by entering the new perceptual stage of 3A.

Other reasons for getting into the Work Addiction Cycle include not recognizing your limits or underestimating your true limits. If you perceive the work to be less than it really is, you can easily become a victim. Before you know it you have overcommitted yourself. Inaccurate perceptual reasoning is the need to add more and more work activities until it is truly too much. Those who create the Cycle in such a manner are often acting from the need to control, lacking trust of other's abilities and possessing the common fear of delegating by believing that the work will be not be successfully accomplished. Whatever the reason, the reality of the situation is incorrectly perceived and thus time and efforts are inappropriately allocated.

On the other hand, some Motivators place perceptual limitations on what they can accomplish in a particular period. When they approach those limits of too much work and their desire for more pushes them past their self imposed perceptual limits. Instead of stretching their perceptions, the Cycle's negative aspects overpower them. At first, they see themselves as busier than others, they may even be proud of themselves because they can feel superior to others. Then as their old perception of "this is beyond me" takes over, they start to become fatigued and enter Stages 3B through 5. They are trapped until they expand their mental mind set of how much they can handle and need to handle by themselves.

MOTIVATORS' PERCEPTIONS OF THE CYCLE

Perhaps you'll learn what this Motivator learned: "Personally, what I've learned about myself has to do with being driven; there was something that I had to prove in terms of my own worth of identity and the way that I proved it was by job performance and accomplishments.....So my basic goal was to live in a way that I could protect myself from being hurt by intense rejection." Whatever the root reason for becoming a Work Addict, to free yourself, you must discover it, analyze it, develop new attitudes about yourself and behave differently.

A wise Motivator gave us her perspective of the Work Addiction Cycle: "A large number of people get caught up in Stage Two. If you go through Stage One, survive and you don't get yourself on an even keel in Stage One, then you move to Stage Two. You take on more and more and sometimes you see that as status. The fatter your attache case is the better person you are, the more important you are.....They can't get along without me. The more I do, the better I feel. I think that's a very honest stage. The challenge is to recognize it and move out of it before you get into all these (mental and physical energy levels)....If you accept yourself as you are, you don't get down into Three and Four...you come through one and two, you'll recognize two for what it is. That's a false motivation, I think. It's self-motivation. It's different than self-actualization. The idea of just keeping going to satisfy your ego, you are caught in Stage Two...This fifth one, there's no satisfaction. You're on an ego trip and you're going in the wrong direction and you don't even know it. I doubt if there's any real satisfaction, if you recognize what real personal satisfaction is. There isn't a lot of it after you leave Stage One....You're losing your contact with your family and your friends and so forth. There's something wrong with the motivation from Two, Three, Four and Five. Wouldn't you say?"

We agree there is something wrong with the motivation. The motivation might have been correct to begin with but the circumstances sometimes trap the individual into moving through these stages. Once you get started and are into Stage 3B, there's very little hope of turning back without pain. The pain may come from continuing or it may be from saying "no" or "let's slow down."

The causes as we have discussed in this chapter vary from Motivator to Motivator. An interview with one Motivator provide some additional insight into the human psyche and how to be healthy in avoiding it: "Don't blind yourself to other mountains. I think that"s what keeps you from being burnt out. But you don't want to do it at such a pace, that it's frantical. I saw a wonderful saying that said, 'Don't be humble, you're not that great...from God to my ear.' Part of that is learning to live with success, so that when people say, "That's quite an achievement, 'you don't say 'Ah, it wasn't anything.' You say 'thank you, I'm pleased with it.'...I'm now 41, but I figure my best years are coming.....I feel that I'm just going to learn more and more. I will get better and better...more powerful...and happier. One of the best things is that I didn't stay in five. I think I'm starting to learn to enjoy success.....There are still things that I still have to learn. When I hit 25, I said, 'oh, I must be an adult,' and I thought 'this is boring, now I know everything.' But you always learn new stuff. Sometimes it is the same lesson in disguise, but I'm always learning new things and that is exciting."

Learning to live with success can be very difficult for the Motivator, who believes in striving for goals. The pursuit of goals can blind the Motivator to personal needs. Instead of working steadily and enjoying life along the way, the Motivator moves full speed ahead. At first, the only enjoyment seems to come from the striving, then later it's power wears off. By that time. the Motivator is fully into the Work Addiction Cycle. Success drives the process, yet when success is achieved, it holds very little warmth. The Motivator in this case doesn't know how to enjoy it, he or she only knows how to achieve it. Success is something to be treasured and reveled in. Motivators who have learned to reward themselves for a successful endeavor, are less likely to be experiencing work addiction.

When we asked Joan Tirak, a religious educator about her perceptions of how to avoid the Work Addiction Cycle, she responded: "I think I understand that it exists. Understand yourself and the characteristics. Pace yourself and balance yourself. Then have the courage to back out on some things, prioritize or delegate a little more or take a look at really where you are."

FORGETTING TO LOVE YOURSELF BEFORE YOU LOVE YOUR NEIGHBOR

Lack of self acceptance and self love can justify for some Motivators their involvement in the later stages of the Work Addiction Cycle. If you truly care for yourself, would you enter the Work Addiction Cycle after you know of its existence? Sure you will. Your knowledge and choice of Stage 3A must be consciously exercised until it becomes a firmly embedded value. And this is tough to do. However, you can't effectively help others if you are not coming from a solid base of self esteem and self acceptance.

DEALING WITH FAILURE

Failure is an experience most Motivators and nonMotivators like to avoid. However, most of us have had to deal with it from time to time. On these rare occasions, we may have failed either in a small way or in large unforgiveable manner (or so we think). Even though failure can have positive benefits, we don't enjoy it. Failure is not fun. It can hurt immeasurably those that it touches. Some people are even scarred for life having experienced one major failure. Experiencing Stage 5A is having failed as well as is returning again and again to drive yourself through Stages 3B, 4 and 5B.

At the very least, the fear of failure resides within many of us as we begin a new project or when we are nearing the finish line of a project. This fear of failure can either stifle us or urge us to move swiftly ahead.

TO AVOID THE WORK ADDICTION CYCLE REQUIRES WORK

Seeing this scenario of pain and accomplishment in the Work Addiction Cycle, some people would diagnose martyrdom and preach moderation. Moderation is such a dirty word to a Motivator. Peers and family often suggest it to the ambitious Motivator. Moderation feels limiting for the Motivator. The Motivator doesn't believe the thrills will be the same with moderation.

Yet, recognizing that the desire to do more is unquenchable is part of the cure. The Motivator must analyze why he or she is susceptible to this Cycle.

The essential question is do we heed our individual cues to pace ourselves or do we rationalize them? We have the potential to do both. It can be helpful to make certain decisions ahead of time...

SELF ANALYSIS QUIZ 2

These are questions to consider about your work, your pace and your potential for entering the Work Addiction Cycle.

1. What deadlines can we live under and for how long?

   - how many major projects can we realistically handle? (now reduce that by 15% because typically we are unrealistic even when we're trying to be realistic)
   - how many patients/clients can you see and still feel motivated?
   - what are you doing to provide yourself with self acceptance?
   - how many 12-16 hour days have you worked consecutively?

2. What will you do the next time you are telling yourself you really have to do it, have to do your best, or better than your best?

   - why do you need to be perceived as someone who has a strong will?

3. If you went through Stages 3B-5 before, what drove you over the edge?

   - what opportunities will you miss by limiting your efforts or delegating?
   - how can you control through managing and not get caught in the trap of doing everything in order to feel in control?
   - do you enjoy being in control of projects? Why do you feel the need to be controlling so much? Do you see the need to control because you need to prove something to somebody or to yourself? Do you truly appreciate your finer points? Can you feel good without being in control of every detail?

4. Do you know your own limits?

   - what perceptual limits have you set regarding the amount of work you can handle?
   - what physical symptoms do you start to have when your body is trying to tell you to reduce your load? What will you do the next time you feel these?

5. If you are working the weekend, do you take time off during the week and create your own weekend?
   - when you finish a big project, do you celebrate and then relax or quickly go on to the next one?
   - have you had a pretty steady period of working and doing a lot during your days and nights?
   - what will you do the next time you have cancelled several consecutive fun activities?

6. What will you do the next time you are feeling a major portion of your life is out of sync with the rest of your life?
   - is the fear of failure strong for you because you're in Stages 4 or 5A?
   - if you fail, do you mentally dislike or beat yourself up?
   - if you fail, can you still like yourself?
   - are you afraid of succeeding and what it will mean to your life?

Answering these questions can help you make appropriate decisions to avoid entering the later stages if you choose to respect your own guidance. They also will be much easier to implement if you have done an analysis of why you are susceptible to being a Work Addict or a Compulsive Worker.

OUR CONCLUSIONS/YOUR CONCLUSIONS?

The question remains if you are currently in or have been in Stages 3B-5, why did you become involved in it? Why did you choose Stage 3B instead of Stage 3A? Search deeply by yourself or with a close analytical friend because the answer may save you from continuing to the ultimate end...physical exhaustion or burn out.

B-3
BREAKING
FREE OF THE
CYCLE

LEAVING THE AMUSEMENT PARK BEHIND

For a Motivator work in Stages 1 and 2 can be like an amusement park. There are many thrilling rides to experience and enjoy. We start out by running the rides and end up riding the exciting rides ourselves. A tremendous high comes from being productive and seeing people change and grow because of what we have said or done. As we run from the rocket ride to the tilt-a-whirl, we all need to line up for a ride on the double ferris wheel to see the world beyond the amusement park. Beyond the amusement park fence is the balance of our lives. It can be a fertile valley with the rich green foliage of psychological, emotional and spiritual growth or a barren desert. Which of these scenarios represents your life beyond work?

How long has it been since you meditated about something other than work? When was the last time you sat and did nothing for more than 3 minutes? How long has been since you enjoyed a meal with family or friends and talked about everyday occurrences? When did you last relax for an hour in the sun or in a favorite chair gazing at a roaring fire?

We delude ourselves if we don't have this richness inside prior to the act of giving and motivating while revolving around in the tilt-a-whirl or riding the race horse on the high speed merry go round. Often this richness comes from spending priority time with ourselves and discovering we are truly fine people.

Your health and long distance endurance depends on your becoming willing to leave the amusement park behind and enjoy the balance of life. Nature has its points of ebb and flow. Three seasons of growth and development are balanced with a season of rest and recuperation. Healthy Motivators understand the need for this same pattern in their own lives. They know life is learning to enjoy all of the facets of life in and beyond the amusement park, sometimes at full speed and sometimes just coasting along.

BALANCE YOUR WHEELS

We suggest you examine and determine how much of your physical, emotional and mental capability is being tapped by your work or projects. Balancing work in each of these three areas is essential to your continuance as a Motivator. If a project will take from all three areas and 90-100% capacity for each, then you need to recognize the impact this will have on your long term ability to finish your mission. If the project extends over a 3 week period and you know this is your limit for traveling at such a pace, you need to decide how you will adjust without experiencing all the stages. Take time to ask yourself, are you draining your reservoirs?

Typically, Motivators have multiple projects going at times. Take the time to think about the nature of the projects. Are they running at different speeds or will they all need to be finished at the same time? When these projects become overwhelming, problems will occur. In stress reduction, it has been suggested that when you are doing a lot of mental work, balance it with physical work.

Draw your own profile of trouble. Ask yourself questions in the self analysis quiz in the earlier chapter. List your own symptoms in your own Work Addiction Cycle if you've experienced it before. If you have only experienced the early stages, analyze why you stopped there. Then decide to not give yourself permission to go into the later stages. No project is worth the risk of losing your health or enthusiasm.

If you have experienced the later stages of the Work Addiction Cycle, list the negative aspects and consequences of your behavior.

Do some reality testing. If your job is really worth your all, how will you do it if you are exhausted at the end of a Work Addiction Cycle? You won't be able to accomplish your missions if you are not at 100% capacity.

TAKE NOTE:

WHEN YOU ARE WORKING AT
100% CAPACITY FOR 5 DAYS AT 11 HOURS PER DAY = 5 x 11 x 1.00 = 55 hours of work

WHEN YOU ARE WORKING AT
100% CAPACITY FOR 5 DAYS AT 8 HOURS PER DAY = 5 x 8 x1.00 = 40 hours of work

WHEN YOU ARE WORKING AT
40% CAPACITY FOR 5 DAYS AT12 HOURS PER DAY = 5 x 12 x .40 = 24 hours of work

Essentially, this is the Motivator's choice. Working at a lower level of capacity because you've worked too many days and too many hours at 100% capacity. Now you could add two more 12 hour days to the 40% capacity and get the satisfaction 9.6 hours of work. Your body loses its resting time but you will gain almost ten hours more. The choice is yours. There is a good reason for resting on weekends. Your body will show the effects if you don't rest and eventually so will the quality of your work.

Add your own hours and honestly evaluate your effectiveness. Are you cheating yourself and your mission by not resting on weekends? Ask a significant other to give you their opinion as well.

Then ask yourself why you need to control so many details? What need is not being satisfied and why are you trying to fill it by moving into Stage 3B to control more? What might you miss if you delegate or turn away work? What other ways can you still get the work done but by managing instead of doing? What can you do to change your perception about control from management versus control by actively doing, so that you can enjoy the fruits of control i.e., results?

FUN, BALANCE & PACE

Humor is a great curative for Motivators in the early stages. It relaxes and revives our restorative elements. One can not hold two conflicting emotions in our minds at one time, thus reducing the intensity of the negative effects. One of our authors described learning of this while in school. She would sneak off to the library and read humorous books such as Robert Benchley's. She found an hour of laughter reviving and encouraging. Currently, she maintains a file of humor. These files evoke hilarity. Another mental perspective is to consider "Will this matter in 10 years?"

Dr. Harold Ellens, therapist told us about his perspective about managing his life: "I think what a Motivator really does eventually is what a good soldier does, like a successful general. That is progressively, as he sees his strength waning a little, he streamlines the efficiency of his operations. He delegates more. By the time he is able to command more resources to which to delegate, he sets priorities with a little more precision. I am at the point in my life where two or three interesting words have become increasing significant. One of them is anymore. You'd be amazed at the number of things I'm never going to do anymore. You'd be surprised at how many things at age 52, you'll never have to put up with anymore nor never have to worry about anymore. That's wonderful. I'm going to have more fun in the next 10 years at non-work activities. I suppose what I'm doing is progressively fine-tuning my operation. I don't even know for sure whether my productivity will decrease until I'm 70 or so. But if it maintains, it will maintain at a significantly lower expenditure of energy by me. That means there will be a lot of other people who are expending more energy accomplishing what I'm doing."

Another Motivator describes her significant other's decisions about his life thusly: "He worked for a large corporation for twelve years. He knows what it's like to be driven to establish yourself and your creditability, to gain the experience, to be successful, to prove something to yourself. He went through it to the point where he said 'this is enough. I'm going to do do this for myself now' and he left saying 'all I care about is just being able to make as much money as I'm currently making working for this company but being able to do it for myself.' So he set modest expectations. He also felt that it would probably take him three to five years to even be that successful but he made the commitment and now he's doing it. He said the biggest difference now is that he only has to answer to himself. He doesn't have to answer to all of those other people. It has relieved a tremendous amount of pressure for him even though there all kinds of other unique pressures in his work now because there isn't anyone to pass it on to. The burden falls on him. He feels that he is directly in control of what happens."

These comments are from very successful men who have chosen to change their approaches to work and being Motivators. They are less likely to enter the final stages of the Work Addiction Cycle. They control their lives versus these stages controlling them.

In order to avoid or to stop being a Work Addict, the Motivator must recognize he or she is the most important person in his or her world. Essentially the Motivator needs to see and believe in loving self before trying to give to others. This belief must be actively practiced prior to entering Stage 3B of the Work Addiction Cycle. Short of doing that the Motivator needs to find the courage to love himself or herself enough to say "I'm too important" to burn out by continuing in this Cycle. Then he or she can use the suggestions in this chapter and the ones in the last section of the book to eliminate the addictive functions of work.

DETERMINING WHICH OF OUR PERCEPTIONS ARE REAL

The Motivator's characteristics of drive, persistence and dedication to finishing can easily create the perceived need to give the extra effort where none is require.

While writing this book, we experienced the early stages of the Cycle. We suffered the same psychological pain but we were able to avoid the more negative stages. We felt for the most part the collaboration made the process much more enjoyable and more paced. We also were watching each other for symptoms. We also encouraged each other to do relaxing activities like walking, swimming, going to movies and enjoying the company of friends. When we started to move into Stage 3B and 4, we chose to change our perceptions, admit our fears of failure and realize these were normal but allowed us to move back to Stage 3A and control.

When we noticed the early symptoms of tiredness, frenetic pace and minor illness, we began to nurture each other. We helped each other by talking about our experiences and feelings. Sometimes, we would confront each other about the sad truth of the situation. Yet, it still remained with us to decide how to handle our situations. You can do the same with a fellow Motivator or ask a supportive friend to monitor your behavior.

As a Motivator you have a responsibility to take care of yourself in order to achieve your mission and goals. Burn out is not only nonproductive but a disservice to the mission. Give yourself permission to rest and relax. Productivity is often measured by quality not quantity. Motivators forget about this, sometimes. You may need to take a vacation so you can come back and be more productive. You may want to check the your perceptions of reality. Are you limiting yourself or creating feelings of being overwhelmed when you're really able of handling more?

LISTEN TO THOSE LITTLE VOICES

The symptoms are just beginning when you feel a little bit overwhelmed. Listen to the little voice inside saying "Hey kid, wait a minute, you're biting off an awful lot here." The other little voice inside may be saying, "But you can handle it, you've done it before." Beware of your dual nature. Recognize the cautionary voice may be your friend. Realize the overly positive voice may be your enemy in this situation because it's encouraging you to do more than you should. Recognize you could be harming yourself immeasurably by experiencing Stages 3B-5.

Our nature of striving encourages us to listen to the voice that suggests we keep going even though it's really an over anxious voice. Sometimes we believe the "Go for it!" voice is the good voice and the other is the bad voice. It may be the complete opposite.

Other symptoms to watch for include becoming accident prone, juggling appointments, which can destroy one's credibility in the long run. We need to check our performance, is everything up to snuff. Our health may be at stake.

The essential question is do we heed our individual cues to pace ourselves or do we rationalize them? We have the power to do both. We have the power to help others and we have the power to help ourselves.

Have you used any of these phrases in the last week?

"I've got to"
"As soon as this is over, I will do something different"...(different meaning...prescriptive or nurturing)
"Yes but,"
"I promise I will do this other activity I have been putting off when I finish this"

What similar rationalization phrases come to your mind?

These questions indicate you either have an inaccurate perceptual problem or your motives for doing what you're doing lie at deeper level than what your activities can sustain. Check yourself out...are you seeking to be accepted, prove you can do something greater than you've done before, or trying to control so you can feel good about yourself?

NURTURE YOURSELF, YOU DESERVE IT

In addition to analyzing your behavior, there are a number of ways to avoid the negative stages of the Cycle. Some nurturing remedies can safeguard you along the way if you will decide to apply them.

Time outs provide needed breaks for rest. When you take a time out, you don't fill your time with chores and errands. You may take a nap or going shopping for pleasure not necessities. You may read a novel or do whatever you want to do, not what you think you're supposed to do.

You may decide to reduce your standards on neatness at home and the office until the crunch period is over. Some of these maintenance functions will wait for you. Instead of doing your hair or nails yourself, you purchase those services. Buy services such as lawn mowing, snow removal, car wash, and house painting to give yourself the time to work and enjoy resting. These are ways to self nurture and remove portions of your burdens. These are all ways to exist at peak performance.

If you have two major projects, ask yourself if you can reduce your efforts on one project for awhile. Some Motivators have done the opposite and experienced Stages 3B-5. The result was that they had to take time to recuperate after Stage 5.

MOTIVATOR MISSION CONTROL

When work takes priority over physical, mental, emotional, and psychological needs, the Motivator has turned himself or herself into a self sacrifice. Self sacrificing on a steady basis indicates a general lack of high self esteem.

One suggestion came from Dr. Douglas Sanders, Ph.D. about ways to avoid burn out: "I think there are ways to avoid burn out. Part of that is just looking at the time of year that you have been working on a particular project and saying 'hey, let me have a vacation and get away from this or let's eliminate this.' It gives you a chance to get away and think more clearly. Divorcing yourself from the situation for a certain extent for a period of time is a way to avoid burn out. I find if you evaluate the quality of your own work and you say...'well this is getting done, but it's not getting done as well as I would like it to'...that's probably a time when you need to get away and get a breath of fresh air. It may be as little as a four day week-end. If a Motivator or anyone can look at their output and see that they are not doing their job quite as well as they need to, then that's the time to divorce yourself, even though there's a schedule coming along that you've got to meet. Sometimes even a day or an afternoon is enough." The Motivator needs to take short vacations and rest periods to continue to perform at a high energy level. The Motivator can do far more if he or she is well rested. The ultimate good of the mission is protected by protecting the ultimate good of the Motivator.

For some reason, the unhealthy Motivator thinks the mission is more important than his/her own needs. One author says "Hogwash!" to that. The mission is important but it takes second place when the Motivator is hurting.

Mission control is out of control when the Motivator is self destructing.

Motivators, who find themselves susceptible to this addiction, need to find the Motivator Mission Control, a reality-testing person to help them. It could be another Motivator or a significant other. You need someone who will tell you, you're showing the signs and tell you to consider what you're doing to yourself. This can be helpful, if you give yourself permission to consider how to control the overwhelming projects before they become overwhelming. Sometimes, if you make a decision you can prevent or eliminate the nastiness of the addiction. You may need a tremendous amount of will power or the stern supportive help from a friend.

Most Motivators have an idea of whether a project or a job will be exceedingly demanding. Prior to entering into a potential addictive situation, the Motivator should consider ways to check his or her progress.

Make a contract with your Motivator Mission Control person to talk about your progress, once a month. You can assign a date for this ahead of time. If you have to reschedule a date twice, this is a sure sign to stop and think about what you're doing to yourself.

One person commented upon using this strategy, that the first time she resented being taken away from her work. Overall, however, she appreciated it because it was helpful to gain perspective and rest.

Sometimes we have to be brought kicking and screaming away from our missions. We are afraid we'll lose something or valuable time if we stop.

The significant other can drag us off to the movies or to dinner in order to get us to rest. The pause may be all we need to recharge.

One of the authors of this book experienced a concussion during one of the busier periods. For her to slow down, was not only psychologically difficult it was something she refused to do. Several days later, she was emotionally as well as physically in pain. She found it painful to think and laid in bed for 4 days trying not to think. This author experienced many fears. She worried not only about not returning to her normal intellectual capacity but how much wasn't being written for the book. By the fourth day, she was convinced she would get well and stopped being afraid of not getting well. She also knew being healthy again was more important than anything else. She admits to having entered Stage 3B of the Work Addiction Cycle, just prior to the injury. She had to slow down until she recovered her health. She became her own Mission Control.

One executive suggested to us breaking the Cycle by "getting the hell out of town for a week, go on a trip. Changing environments, giving the head a chance to relax and recreate the vision."

These are all ways to value yourself and maintain your self esteem at a high level. Doing less and getting more enjoyment from what you do by savoring it versus gulping more work can help you gain higher levels of self esteem. The basis for self esteem rests in the conclusion that you're really a fine person.

SUMMARY

The reasons as we've discussed are varied for entering the Work Addiction Cycle, the solutions need to match the causes. If it's a perceptual problem, the perceptions must be examined and changed. If the Cycle is truly caused by too much work, the Motivator must alter his or her behavior. If the cause resides at a deeper level relating to self acceptance, then the Motivator needs to seriously examine his/her motives and determine whether entering the Work Addiction Cycle will exacerbate the unfulfilled need or supply it appropriately. The Motivator who likes to control his/her life and others' lives in order to feel superior is probably doing a disservice to many people most importantly himself/herself.

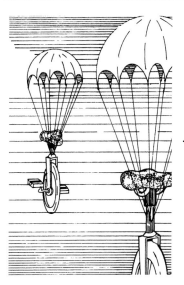

B-4
HOW TO BEAT THE FEAR OF FAILURE

Literature and art have presented failure's many facets and its survivors. One such example is exemplified in a limited edition print by Donald Vann, a famous contemporary native American artist. Vann has painted a picture of a Cherokee indian warrior returning from a hunt during a snow storm. We see him walking into camp as if we are walking silently behind him. He returns with only his horse to his high mountain camp.

If we are the warrior coming home empty handed even though we have given our best effort what do we do? How can we face those who believed in us, now that we have failed? How do we face ourselves and continue to believe we can rise up and succeed the next time? The answers are simple to state but, require us to have faith, courage and an extra amount of driving persistence even when we think our reserves have been depleted

ON THE ROAD TO RECOVERY

THE FIRST STEPS TO DEALING WITH FAILURE

Failure doesn't have to stymie you, here are eight steps to remedying the situation.

1. Recognize it and allow yourself to feel the grief for awhile, a day at most.

When, not if, we fail, we have the choice to feel or to avoid feeling for awhile. Naturally, we have done our best, but somehow we have missed the mark. Failure painfully reminds us that we are vulnerable and can't control our lives to the extent we wish we could. Failure is something we would like to avoid and yet it happens. Of course, at first we wish circumstances were different. We would like to forget the situation. A sense of grief and disappointment is a natural reaction to a seemingly hopeless situation. To say no one enjoys this stage of remorse for a lost hope is truly an understatement. The pain can seem searingly immense and unrelenting.

We hurt badly. As Motivators, we are people who feel deeply, whether it's ecstasy or sorrow. Feeling pain is probably healthy for us. We tend to feel deeply, unless we have turned off the emotional side. Turning off and not facing it only delays the healing. Delaying also robs us of the benefits of learning about ourselves, what went wrong and how we can make the future even better. Sooner or later, we must come to the point of releasing the grief. For it is unmistakably grief that we feel.

Crying provides a release for some of us. For others, letting out anger or going for a long fast walk or run seems to help. Whatever your particular method, dealing with it provides relief from the anguish you are experiencing.

One Motivator has discovered a helpful activity. After understanding it, she visualizes packaging the failure and pain into a garbage bag and emptying the trash. From that point, when she feels the pain, she reminds herself that it went out with the trash. She then thinks new thoughts and begins a new direction.

2. Drop your membership in the "Time to Mentally Beat Myself Up Club."

The immediate reaction of many Motivators is to join the "Time to Mentally Beat Myself Up Club." Expecting continual or nearly continual perfection, these Motivators feel demoralized by their lowered level of performance. The "Time to Mentally Beat Myself Up Club" is the one we join when we silently tell ourselves how rotten we are and how bad our mistake was. Some of us willingly beat ourselves for several days or longer.

To discontinue this practice, go into an empty room by yourself, close the doors. Then say aloud all the negative things you've been saying silently. Start out softly and continue while increasing your volume. Exaggerate a bit. Feel bad? Terrific. Now, you have abused yourself long enough. But take no longer than 15 minutes to do this and preferably 5 minutes. Now as you leave the room think of one your positive traits. The next time you think about this mistake and how bad you are, stop yourself. Say "Stop!" forcefully yet silently and replace the negative thought with a positive thought about yourself or what you're currently doing. Realize you have punished yourself enough and it's time to move on. Continuing to beat yourself mentally is a waste of time and energy. If you continue to be actively involved in this Club, failure has robbed you of your potential.

Dropping out of the "Time to Mentally Beat Myself Up Club," takes discipline and is not accomplished overnight. It took one of the authors six months of practice to limit herself to two blows, but it is well worth the time she gained feeling good about herself and pursuing new goals and growth.

3. Ask what can I learn from this failure?

Analyze the reasons you failed. Analyzing what went wrong can produce new ideas and new exciting directions. It's challenging to examine yourself and the situation to determine the causes of failure and how to avoid it next time.

The reasons for failure never fully lie in one camp. There are usually numerous causes.

Once you feel you have examined all the potential causes, then, ask yourself, "what will I do differently next time?" This sets a new pattern for a more successful try.

There is an old story about Thomas Edison, which has helped many individuals in our seminars. It was told to us by a seminar participant many years ago. It helps put failure in its proper perspective.

It seems a reporter was walking with Edison through the back door of his lab when he noticed all the junk of broken inventions. The reporter was dumbfounded, after all, Edison was the great inventor. How could he have made such a huge number of failures. So he asked Edison why he had made all those mistakes. Edison replied simply.."Those aren't mistakes, those are just 1001 ways not to make the light bulb."

We chuckle at this story but the point is clear when we fail we have an opportunity to learn from our mistakes. Most people mature quickly after experiencing failure. The hardest kind of failure is when we've failed but we can't seem to understand what we did wrong. It's not whether we fail or not but if and how we pick ourselves up afterwards.

If we can realize that a failure is only a minor setback, we have the potential to succeed and make the success far sweeter. Failure brings hope for us once we've agreed to believe in ourselves again. After experiencing the pain, we must choose a new direction or move back up the mountain that we just fell from. It is never too late to begin again.

Typically, Motivators learn from failure and push on. Some had an early experience with failure. Strangely, this experience created the direction of their motivational mission. As a result, they wish to express the value of their experience to others in order to prevent others from experiencing the same kind of fear.

While we were editing this chapter, we happened to talk with a therapist in the Pittsburgh Airport's cafe line. He was reading a book titled Failures In Family Therapy. After a quip asking about whether the book's focus was failure in the families or the therapist's failure, this unknown therapist made an insightful comment about failure in general. He said "Sometimes it's easier to learn from your failures that it is from your successes." Perhaps failure squarely faces us and demands we look at our strengths and weaknesses. Those of us who truly learn from failure take the time to examine both of these more clearly than when success distracts us from viewing our weaknesses. When we fail, we must be able to see both to gain a new resolve to continue or begin again. It is one of the secrets of failure that the growth experience directly related to failure can motivate the Motivator to go on. Most Motivators never allow a failure to finish them off. They find a hidden reserve to move ahead.

4. Recognize the answer to "what do I do now?" may not be readily apparent.

Relax. Perhaps, choose a short term goal to rest up for awhile. If the answer is not clear, don't proceed too quickly to the next available goal just so you'll feel comfortable. This is your time to regroup your wagons in a circle to plan a offensive strategy. So take the time to rest and then plan but not until you're ready emotionally.

5. Write about your feelings and thoughts or talk with several friends.

This is a strategy to deal with your emotions in a deeper way beyond Step 1. If you can write about your feelings in a journal or on sheet of paper, it can help you to handle the pain. Talking with friends can be especially beneficial to getting some solid feedback from those who can help you the most.

6. Wait until your enthusiasm returns before planning alternative directions, then choose very carefully for success.

Your enthusiasm will return. Motivators are seldom down for a long time unless they have burned out. One of the unique aspects of being a Motivator is possessing a renewable source of enthusiasm and energy. Sometimes it just takes a little longer to rediscover your source. Once you do, you'll be okay.

7. Reward yourself for being you.

Go to a movie, read a book, or do something active... some form of physical exercise. You are rewarding yourself for being you, not for failing. It becomes a means of accepting yourself and your mistakes. After all, you are an acceptable person, one who is loved and respected. The basis of this action is revealed in the appreciation of the next step.

8. Remember even if you failed, you are still an acceptable person.

The failure was a behavior. You are still a good person. You failed. But now is the time to realize who you are is not dependent upon how well you succeed. You are not a title or a job, you are you and that's more than enough.

It's been said that the greatest love you can have is to love yourself. If you can do that, you have the keys to a successful life. For even when you fail, you have the elements necessary to succeed again.

A FALSE SENSE OF FAILURE

For some Motivators, slowing down or when circumstances create a slow down, they experience a false sense of failure. The nature of the Motivator is to desire continual development or progress. Challenges or obstacles tend to stimulate the Motivator to become an opportunity developer. Typically breaking new ground excites the Motivator. If no new challenges are in the near future, sometimes Motivators think they have failed in some way.

One Motivator mentioned, "If you're not using your ability or talents, you feel like you've failed. You ask yourself, 'what's wrong with me?' Because I see myself in the role of a people gardener I like to see people blooming and growing. When they blossom from new knowledge they have acquired from me, I feel a pleasing sense of pride. If there's a storm in the process and the blossom of learning dies, I sometimes feel guilty."

It's important to remember during these times to tell ourselves, we have no control over another person's success or failure. Perhaps we're aware of this fact cognitively but we tend to forget during a crisis. Everyone has a choice of what to do with the advice received. Motivators are able to help some maybe even many but complete control is never an appropriate goal.

Over stimulation can also create an exhausted Motivator, who doesn't know the meaning of quit. One trainer commented, "Life is not a a series of multiple choice questions, it's thinking. As a thinking and giving person, I give out great amounts of energy. This energy of giving out needs to be replaced instead of just depleted. I often feel mentally satisfied but physically drained from the motivational experience. It saddens me that I experience a physical failure but I have learned I need to quit and recuperate."

Another aspect of failure seems to result from the "symbiotic" relationship between the Motivator and the needy. One Motivator noted that "we need them as much as they need us. When this interaction is missing we may feel we are failing in some way." The reality may be that this false sense of failure is a sign that it's time to rest or to seek a new goal.

Most healthy Motivators will make course corrections. It can be perceived as a new challenge to conquer. Failure of the preceding types can be the Motivator's best friend. Often, the failure will bring a whole new direction or a new twist on the original plan. Work slow downs thus provide the impetus for the Motivator to reconsider previous choices.

Regardless of the obstacles, most Motivators will persevere to the end. A slow down obstacle gives the Motivator needed time to consider new directions.

THE PERPETUAL POTENTIAL GAME

Another type of failure occurs when the Motivator is helping a person with permanent potential. The PERMANENT POTENTIAL PERSON has many fine qualities but chooses not to use them. Some Motivators find this difficult to accept. They are more understanding of those who don't have great talents.

We all make choices about goals and the amount of effort we can give to them. The need for job security or family needs can retard the growth of the Permanent Potential Person from becoming a fully operative Motivator. Other Permanent Potential People fear failure and choose to play it safe by seeking lesser goals, which are sure bets.

Unfortunately, the Permanent Potential Person wastes the time of the Motivator, who is attempting to influence him or her to realize his/her full potential. The illusion is that with the right motivation, the Permanent Potential Person will accomplish great things. The Motivator is challenged by the illusion to motivate. The nature of an illusion tempts the Motivator into wasting his or her time trying to influence where there is the lack of true desire to risk and become more in the direction suggested by the Motivator.

IF YOU ARE A HOME RUN HITTER, YOU HAVE A HIGH STRIKE OUT POTENTIAL

Hank Aaron hit the most home runs of any baseball player. Yet, he also had the dubious record of having the most strike outs of any player. It's been said if you aim high, you have a greater potential to fail and fail in major way. Choosing the safer road can assure success but at what price? The loss of "what might have been" is equally great. Each person must choose which road to walk for this life time.

The choice is never easy. Choosing the more difficult road of believing in one's self and pushing forward by taking risks when others suggest caution, can lead to an early failure, but also has a great potential for long term success. Taking risks doesn't mean that you won't be afraid. Fear is a very natural part of being willing to risk. You are risking the loss of your immediate self esteem if you fail. Those who fear failure the most can easily let it control them or they can choose to face the fear by taking a chance. Thus they learn a greater lesson that fear once it is faced can no longer grip you like it did. You've transcended its power and you're free to be all that you can be.

Responding to a personal unemployment crisis, one Motivator describes her experience with her father. "I was pretty depressed about my opportunities. Nothing was readily available. My Dad responded to my need for sympathy by telling me that I had achieved the best I could expect. Further he indicated I might have to accept something less. I remember crying and then feeling angry enough to say to him 'I can't accept less, I want something better. I need your encouragement now more than ever. I need to hear positive words. I want to hear you say that you believe I can go on and that I'm good and I should hang in there for the best.' Perhaps my tears and plea for help startled him. From that point on he has been always supportive of my efforts."

She continued by saying "I did go on to obtain a great position, which led me into a new career that I had never considered. Having set this expectation of I would not accept anything less than what I had had, I not only gained more, but the best. I sincerely believe if you set an expectation in your mind, circumstances will occur to fulfill it. My expectation was I was not going to be an under-employed individual.

I have found that some people will accept less than what they deserve because of seemingly unsurmountable experiences because it's all that is currently available or it's all they can believe of themselves. The worse aspect of this occurs when a someone close to them encourages them to take less because they love them and want them to be financially secure.

Depression has helped me to realize when I need to shift gears for something new in my life. Instead of feeling sorry for myself for failing, I needed my father to shake me up a little. Without knowing what he was doing, he helped me to recognize an essential truth for me, **NEVER ACCEPT LESS THAN THE BEST BECAUSE IF YOU KEEP LOOKING, THE BEST IS WAITING TO BE DISCOVERED.**

FAILURE PROVIDES THE NECESSARY RESPITE

Sometimes, we need what seems like a failure in order to rest, so we can contemplate about the next mission. If handled correctly, failure can be a fortuitous experience leading to new and better goals. Failure can help us to find a new direction that provides even more meaning for our lives.

The fallow or dormant Motivator can be the result of physical exhaustion, burnout or Stage 5A or 5B in the Work Addiction Cycle. This is truly a failure because the Motivator has forgotten the number one rule of taking care of self before the mission. Total depletion of your resources is ultimately a sad state of affairs for your mission. Without your full energy behind it, your mission suffers.

One optimistic Motivator noted "Some of us have to experience the depths of despair in order to appreciate the ecstasy of life." Perhaps it's true that we really know how to appreciate success because we know how emotionally painful failure is. So much so it sometimes seems like a miracle when we experience success having paid our dues through failure.

ANOTHER SIDE OF FAILURE...DEMOTIVATORS

They're everywhere, even mingled among the successes. Demotivators may be people, environments, circumstances or comments. But, they're discouraging because they are the antithesis of Motivators and motivational factors. They lurk about to poison the positive attitudes of others. If they go undiscovered, even a Motivator becomes less optimistic and demotivated. Many times we are unaware of their existence because they disguise their poison as potions of realism.

To help you discover the Demotivators in your life, consider these questions:

1. What kinds of people demotivate me or discourage me?

2. What kinds of environments at work demotivate me or discourage me?

3. What past circumstances have demotivated me or discouraged me from pushing ahead?

4. What kinds of comments (sarcastic or others) demotivate me or discourage me?

Everyone has pet peeves, we're not discussing these here. We're talking about what can reduce or lessen your motivation or hinder you psychologically from moving ahead with your desires or goals. A Demotivator can be a distraction or a deflator depending upon its severity and your level of motivation. Sometimes a Demotivator in the early life of a Motivator challenges the Motivator's inner will. In fact some of the Motivators, we interviewed told us of people who inadvertently channeled them into professional directions they wouldn't have probably considered.

This book's cover designer and illustrator, Kent Ver Planck told us about an experience with his second grade teacher. "What really got me involved in art was a teacher that I had in second grade, who wouldn't put anything of mine on the bulletin board. If my art work wasn't on the bulletin board, I was absolutely ashamed and embarrassed. I would go home and tell my family. So my mother would go and tell this teacher 'You've got to put something of his on the bulletin board.' She refused. I tried everything to get something up. She would constantly tell me, my stuff was just not good enough to put on the bulletin board. She told me 'I had no talent as an artist and to just give it up.' It kept making me want to do more. Most of the time when someone has told me I can't do something, it has made me want to do it more badly."

So the effect of a Demotivator doesn't have to be negative. It can work out for the good of the Motivator. Finding the silver lining in the clouds of a demotivational situation can take years or be difficult at best to discover. Accepting the situation, using it to your advantage or choosing not to surrender to the demotivator can produce a strong will with much leavening power. Either way, a Motivator seems to use it to his/her advantage in the long run. Rarely is a Motivator overcome unless there is a far greater opportunity about to be discovered.

Environments that are Demotivators are much more difficult to change. Some work place environments can be depressive because of others' attitudes and behaviors, the physical conditions, organization's goals and culture, and the pressures of having to work. If you're not in a powerful position, your choices are limited in number but not in the degree of influence you allow them over your attitudes.

First of all, you have the choice to leave or stay. If you choose to stay, you can look at the environment and ask "how can I make this a better place?" What can you add to make it more pleasant and more motivating? How can you change your perceptions of what is happening? What can you concentrate upon that makes you happy rather than sad? What can you enjoy about your work? If you concentrate on the advantages versus the negatives, you can lessen the impact of the Demotivators. No situation has the right to get the best of you if you remember to look for what's best in the situation. Certain circumstances such as failure, politics, lack of money and other occurrences can be discouraging. The key to alleviating their demotivational pain is perceiving them as temporary situations pointing to the need for more motivation or creative answers. We've discussed how to handle failure. Politics in the offices exist in every work situation. The strategies for coping vary depending upon the situation. Staying on the winning side may not be in the plan for long term growth of the Motivator. Sometimes, losing at office politics forces you in a new direction. Again the key is how can you turn a perceived disadvantage into an advantage? Lack of money can cause you to proceed in new directions to gain the money. Or you begin to appreciate the blessings you have even if it is only that you are alive. And that's a wonderful start.

Dealing with Demotivator comments such as sarcasm often requires the Motivator to exercise restraint and patience. Others sometimes envy Motivators or have great difficulty understanding them. Sarcasm or other demotivational comments are meant to bring the Motivator within the understanding or acceptance of these people. In a backward way, the person is telling the Motivator, they are admired but need to be brought down a peg or two so the Motivator's behavior is within reach of being copied. We are a society that wants heroes but we want those close to us to be like us. Heroes can be difficult to live with because they are different and seemingly better. It's a strange phenomenon, one that is difficult to work with the first time around. Understanding and recognizing that the person making the comments lacks self acceptance and probably needs acceptance can help you turn the situation into an opportunity to help someone.

Ignoring them is your last resort if showing them kindness doesn't work. Let them make their comments, but you can replace their negative statement with a positive one in your mind.

HOW CAN A DEMOTIVATOR CHANGE INTO A MOTIVATOR?

By desire and commitment to change, a Demotivator can become a Motivator. Recognizing the need to change can be the first step in achieving this metamorphist. Being a Demotivator is a drag after awhile. Most people wish to be happy. A Demotivator is someone who thinks it's appropriate to be critical of others and their methods. Coming from an anti-establishment bias, they think by criticizing others, they are perceived to be better. After all, critiquing is a a sign of superiority, right? Not necessarily, usually it leads to dissatisfaction and frustration. **PEOPLE WHO ARE DEMOTIVATORS ARE NOT VERY POPULAR.** People don't like to be around Demotivators because their behaviors are so negative and energy depleting, thus creating a miserable environment. Even though they may like people and want to be around people who are happy, they easily bring other's spirits down. They may even disguise their unhappiness as being realists. This kind of reality holds out no comfort for the Demotivator or others.

We've all experienced a situation like the following one that a Motivator described. "On Friday, I was very happy and excited about the weekend. On Friday night, a 'friend' from out of town arrived for a weekend of fun...except he forgot to bring it with him. He was full of negatives. His work life was in a turmoil, the clients weren't as happy as he would have liked with his work. His long term relationship was in trouble because he was spending too much time working. He was upset with the airlines, the government and every one who treated him in a less than appropriate manner. By the end of the weekend of partying, I was beat, I felt like a ton of bricks had been laid on my head. It was several days before I was able to shake his negativity off." This man was a Demotivator through and through. Unfortunately, he probably doesn't realize the wake of damage he leaves behind him.

Typically, Demotivators are pessimistic people who claim to be realists. Afterall, how many people do you know who would admit to being a pessimist? They are pessimistic about themselves and others. They are deflators, who go around putting pins in others people's bubbles of enthusiasm and hope. They accomplish it all so easily through verbal and nonverbal methods. It can be a power play to make the Motivator think he or she is stupid to be "emotionally up." Demotivators may be seeking attention because they aren't happy and they want to feel better. (Misery loves company!)

They may truly believe they are being realistic by cautioning you about your new ideas or your desires. Unfortunately, this misguided pessimism discourages others from being around them. They are hurting others by short changing them from the enjoyment of dreaming, planning and strategizing. Managers who are Demotivators create lackluster employees and usually lose the best people. Managers/supervisors who greet new ideas with "I'll check into it" or give no response are certainly candidates for the Demotivator category. They cause stress in the work place for all those around them, especially the Motivators. It's very stressful to work for or work with someone who is acting in a demotivating way.

One seminar participant shared a story illustrating the Demotivator's perspective. The people in "Hell" were all sitting around long tables but they couldn't eat because their hands were bound to the ends of five foot long spoons. They moaned and complained loudly about the situation. Light years away the people in "Heaven" were sitting down to similar tables holding the same type of spoons. Their reality was the same but they handled it quite differently. They had learned to adjust to the situation by feeding each other.

One of the most wasteful activities is gossiping. Most people gossip to some extent, yet the Demotivator knows nothing else to discuss. Everything is wrong at work, no one knows how to do it right except it would be different if the Demotivator were in charge. A stark reality is that it might not be any better if they were in charge because they know how to find fault but don't know how to improve situations with their own ability. It makes the Demotivator feel good to be able to recognize his/her superiority. Unfortunately, this perspective provides an extremely narrow view of the world and limits one from seeing the beauties in being different. Everyone has something good to share with others.

EVEN DEMOTIVATORS CAN CHANGE

If you think you are a Demotivator and you wish to change into a Motivator, you can. Change is never totally easy. For those of us who have changed from Demotivators into Motivators, it has meant a long road. For some it has involved therapy sessions. For others it has required tremendous will power and discipline to turn negative thoughts into positive thoughts.

One needs to look upon the good things in the work environment and think about these. The prospective Motivator may find it helpful to take a few minutes to think about what you like at work or can be grateful for.

Identify the factors that demotivate people in general. Then check yourself against those factors, are there areas where you could improve. Then plan a systematic pattern for change. Don't be too hard on yourself, it takes time to change your way of being. You can become a more positive person by working at it. Work on improving your own self esteem by noticing and writing down the things you do well or the positive traits you exhibit. At first it might seem to be an unnatural state to be up or high on life.

FAILURE IS A MATTER OF PERCEPTION

Remember, you have only failed completely if you stop trying. It's never too late to begin again. If you start over or you are moving toward success. Failure can be endured or used to your advantage.

Consider the story about the man who failed as a businessman, went on to be a surveyor, only to lose his surveying tools. He became a lawyer, who was shunned by his colleagues at a famous trial. He ran for public office numerous times and lost most of them. Served as a U.S. Senator then lost to another candidate. Later, he had the gall after many failures and experiences of depression to run for the Presidency and win. Abraham Lincoln is a famous example of a person, who knew what it was to fail but he also knew it was his destiny to continue trying.

Is the voice of realism any louder for you than it was for him?

SECTION C:
REVVING UP YOUR POWER TO MOTIVATE AS A MANAGER

C-1
IGNITING YOUR POWER TO MOTIVATE

WANTED: Motivated person who is willing to learn about self and others to a greater degree than the general population. Salary commensurate with your goals and drive, can be unlimited. Must have the ability to think effectively. Need to be a self starter who enjoys performing a life time mission of influencing others. If you possess the ability to create an illusion that produces magical responses within others, you've got what it takes for this position. Plenty of perks given to the person who can consistently exceed others' expectations. Contact Motivators Anonymous for placement, 477-2RPM.

Why would you want to be a Motivator? Obviously, the benefits outweigh the disadvantages. Motivators enjoy extensive benefits and privileges that usually compliment their talents, responsibilities and achievements.

You may be asking what are the benefits of being a Motivator? Even Motivators ask that question from time to time. Let's examine this question more fully.

FOR THE FUN OF IT

Motivators' careers provide many opportunities to have a lot of fun. Work is definitely not drudgery. In fact, most Motivators say they thoroughly enjoy their life's work. Some even charge through life achieving great works. Others step cautiously providing needed value to a few people within their sphere of influence.

The old proverb of getting more than you give is probably a driving force of the Motivator's activities. He or she might not always be thanked or physically rewarded. However, intrinsic rewards usually keep the healthy Motivator moving forward.

Motivators feel good about working and about giving to others. Some told us they felt a tremendous amount of self satisfaction from being Motivators. There's a sense of pride connected with helping others and motivating them to do more than they originally thought possible.

THE THRILL OF LEARNING

If you are a Motivator, then you're probably in a continual state of learning. Motivators tend to learn in unorthodox ways. They learn from talking or listening to other Motivators, from their own experiences, by reading, watching television, and listening to tapes as well as from more traditional methods. They also learn by analyzing everything. Indeed, they learn from everything. Motivators love to experience and then integrate the learning from the experience, afterward. Part of being self actualized is perpetually learning. Motivators are typically open to learning new ideas, new theories, new methods, new concepts, new processes and new procedures. They also learn by developing new concepts of their own. In addition, a great portion of the fun of being a Motivator is concluding new aspects about character growth and about life.

From our observations, we have concluded Motivators have a greater capacity to enjoy more of life than the average person who lives for leisure time and the next pay check. Several people have noted they noticed Motivators were happy and usually smiled the majority of the time.

THE JOY OF THINKING

One Motivator noted: "I experience the ups and downs fully because I'm analyzing them. I've always been a person who thought and analyzed. As I grow older, I'm learning a lot about life, myself, and what other values I need to learn from my experience."

Another Motivator commented, "life is exciting as a Motivator, because you are at the center of many projects. Similar in some ways to being in the eye of a hurricane. Everything around you is moving at tremendous speeds while inside you are at peace with yourself. You are enjoying the moments of creation, interaction with others, integrating ideas and concepts and you're at the receiving side of the adulation of those you respect."

For the Motivator who is a trainer, instant gratification is reaped at the end of a seminar. Participants tell the trainer how much they are enjoying the seminar or how useful they feel it is. They love the positive spirit of the Motivator. Typically, they want some of it. People are drawn to the Motivator, hoping some of the magical qualities will rub off. In most cases, these people are seeking inspiration, personal, and professional development skills. Great satisfaction can be derived from such experiences for both the trainer and the participant. The positive comments nourish and enhance the Motivator's positive self concept.

The market demand is large, but the supply of Motivators in our experience seems to be small. Their missions and jobs require a lot of intuitive ability as well as analytical talent. Many of the Motivators, we have met, are whole brain thinkers. Often, their occupations require this ability to use their left and right sides in a balanced way. To motivate, give, influence, and inspire, they need highly developed analytical and intuitive skills. It's probably not surprising that they are aware of the fact that they have special abilities. Most know who they are and have a healthy sense of self esteem.

THE MATERIAL PERKS

The financial benefits for some Motivators are limited only by the desires of how much money they want to make. Their motivation and enthusiasm sell. They seem to instinctually know how to sell a product or a service. Their personalities favorably impact the outcome of their selling ventures.

Other Motivators find their financial security to be sufficient payment for what they give. These Motivators are typically driven more by altruism once the pay check is secure.

FREEDOM TO BE

From the beginning, Motivators are their own persons. They tend to call the shots. They love to design their jobs, thus insuring job satisfaction to maintain themselves for the long haul. Typically, Motivators have the freedom to do what they want to do. Being very independent people, they enjoy their freedom to personally develop unfettered by conventional values.

One Motivator commented that we live in a highly unusual time. Motivators create change in the world and are readily accepted by others more than ever before. Believing in reincarnation, she commented…"I think my mission this time is to pull together these varied experiences and talents that I've had the opportunity to gather and develop over a number of life times and apply them in the wonderful social dynamics of the last part of the 20th century. This is a wonderful time to be alive! There's just so much change going on. It's scary because we may self destruct. Who knows? But it's a wonderful time! There are so many ways to impact on change right now. It's fantastic. This is my chance to pull it all together in a time in history that is very exciting. I feel we are at the cutting edge of some major social change. If I can facilitate that process and help others understand it, then I will have accomplished what I came here to do this time."

We have observed that many Motivators we interviewed were on the cutting edge of their fields. Their zest for new projects and trying new methods and techniques creates tremendous sources of energy for themselves and those around them. They know where they want to go and very little ultimately stops them because of their courage and desire to be all that they can be.

THE GIFT OF OTHERS

Motivators meet wonderful people both as professional peers and the people they help. Often, both groups inspire the Motivator to do more. As a highly social being, the Motivator is obviously stimulated by others.

Motivators enjoy their ability to have deep, intimate conversations with people. Possessing the ability to delve into their own and other's psyches, they proceed where others would not conceive of going. The emotional charge of this is difficult to explain to a nonMotivator. They find it exhilarating to think with others about a variety of topics. As integrators of divergent concepts, they are constantly trying to make sense of a confusing world. As they do this, Motivators motivate other Motivators. Some Motivators have noted that somehow a mental catharsis occurs when Motivators are talking together.

On this subject, one person told us, that "as a Motivator there's a lot of life to have and enjoy as well as people to experience. Some of these people you want a steady diet of, while others are just a little dessert or appetizer. A Motivator can pick and choose people to enjoy. We can choose to leave out the negative people and put the positive people into our lives to help us grow."

THE MISSION AS A BENEFIT

Motivators love to set goals and enjoy fulfilling them. With the accomplishment of their ambitious goals, they receive a heavy load of satisfaction. Their mission and purpose in life gives them direction and pleasure at the same time. They truly can have their cake and eat it too.

One Motivator commented "it's a life long occupation, so you don't have to retire and cut yourself off from your love. Being a Motivator is a process that is useful on and off the job. The tools for self motivation and healing yourself are available to you at any time."

One Motivator explained the behavior of others toward her, "This person that I become when I'm in my Motivator role is a tremendous person, seemingly a 'larger than life' figure. Other's comments vary but the sentiment is the same. They seem to have a heightened view of us. When we cloak ourselves in our motivational guise--we are more impervious to criticism and become invincible in the minds of those we are influencing. Once we are out of that role we shrink back to normal."

Another Motivator identified benefits of the persona in this fashion: "We enjoy work immensely...all the facets of work. Our work tends to fit us like gloves tailored to our hands...a perfect match with our personalities, characteristics and inner beings. I believe Motivators choose work consciously and subconsciously. Our hidden skills are revealed through the work. We are positive about our work because we see the results of our labors and clearly see the change in attitudes and behaviors of those we serve. We even get thanked for what we do and how many people have that opportunity? We enjoy seeing the effects, ie., the mark we have made in people's lives and then seeing them affect other people is a tremendous thrill."

Some Motivators hope to see their messages live on and on. They want to have a major impact on others. They want to affect many, even globally. Their time is limited, but they seem to want to make the most of it. Being somewhat cognizant of this fact, they press ahead with the details of attaining their missions. They are an elite group because not everyone could do it or wants to do it.

Motivators enjoy being Motivators because of these benefits. While the benefits of acting as a Motivator are enticing, they are really a by-product of being a Motivator. People who are or become Motivators do so because of their values, circumstances or an inner desire to make a difference. Becoming a Motivator or recognizing that you are one is the most effective way to realize your power to motivate.

UNLOCK YOUR MOTIVATOR POWER

So you have decided to become a Motivator. You've been told that it feels good, builds healthy minds and improves your sex life. Well, strike that last one, as a Motivator, you probably won't have time.

On a more serious note, before becoming a Motivator, two points of distinction are worthy of consideration. First, a motivated person is not necessarily a Motivator. Secondly, you can be Motivator and not be a manager.

As we have said, Motivators truly care about people and want to impact and improve other's lives. They typically motivate, influence and inspire out of this desire to help.

Most Motivators have chosen to fulfill a mission or recognize having some purpose in this life time which they must accomplish. The existence of this mission or purpose is obvious to those around the Motivator, if not so obvious to him/her. The mission may vary, but it is usually related to achieving some greater good for others.

Typically, the Motivators we interviewed determined they had a mission or a "reason to be" very early in life. The mission's aspects subsequently change over the years, but an underlying goal of giving remains constant. For many, changes occurred in their early twenties when they asked themselves what they wanted to be and do with their lives. The vast majority of Motivators want to leave a mark or want something out of this life beyond the normal comforts of life. Throughout history people have asked "what is le raison d'etre?"....what is a person's reason to be?

Although it may not be readily apparent the answer is fulfilled to a great extent by a major aspect of realizing your power to motivate. To help you get a better handle on it, the rest of this chapter is devoted to this aspect of developing yourself.

SELF ACCEPTANCE SPELLS RELIEF

For many of us, self acceptance is a never ending process. It is not a place or a goal but an open ended process of continuing to see new facets. Ultimately we come to know we're more than alright-- we're outstanding. This aspect of realizing our self worth has many different components and different ways of being expressed. We can continue for a life time discovering the finer points. Unfortunately, some of us never truly appreciate our personal wealth as well as those who know us best do.

Healthy Motivators realize early on that they love to work. Working for some is using their God given thinking abilities and thus they are often in ecstasy when they are working at their life's work.

Many people try to get Motivators to slow down by telling them such things as "you have too many irons in the fire" or "you're trying to juggle too many balls." These well wishers are usually ignorantly impressing their values of mediocrity on the Motivator. It is ridiculous for them to believe they have any effect on the Motivator other than a deflating effect and quickly becoming an annoyance. We speak harshly here because many Motivators have been done a great disservice by the well meaning mediocre masses. They have been given every reason to feel weird because they are different.

The SO CALLED NORMAL PERSON'S values of mediocrity, average speed and lesser quality doesn't fit the Motivator's value system. Motivators must do what they must without worrying about what others think. Motivators love to think and create. They want to do that with the support of love ones but they will continue without it.

Many Motivators start out with a healthy sense of esteem or work up to it in pursuing their mission. Self esteem eludes the mental grasp of so many people. Motivators who develop an early strong sense of their internal beauty are prepared to face monumental tasks in their lives. Others must simply survive the difficulty of growing up in a discouraging period for their families or for world history. Many take these difficulties and become giant oak trees from tiny acorns.

Sense of self esteem is a confident belief in the goodness of your inner nature. If you are a Motivator, you know you're a fine individual with many wonderful characteristics. You can live with the knowledge that not everyone will like you or want to be like you. In fact in your growing up years, you may have been an oddity at times. As you grow and mature, others may have come to appreciate your talents and the inner you.

Whenever you develop a healthy sense of self esteem, you've reached a new plateau. No longer are you in the valley of others' perspectives of you. You have begun a new trail along the plateau's edge to becoming the best you can be and enjoying it thoroughly. What ever you do or believe, you know that you are normal for you. You may seem odd to others, who get a close look at you and note that you are a bit different. Yet, in your heart, you know you are who you should be. It may hurt when others reject you because they can't understand why you have chosen your path. Still, there are others who do understand and love you as you are. More importantly, you are no longer fighting to be you. You just exist and through that existence,many profit by your uniqueness. You have come to realize you are a special person, with gifts and talents that are uncommon.

In Maslow's Hierarchy of Needs terminology you are well on the way to becoming self actualized. You know who you are and you're constantly moving toward becoming all you can be. You have a zest for living and caring about others. You see life as a means to grow and develop you personal strengths. Learning from life's many experiences and enjoying its fullness becomes a significant goal in life. Maturity comes with understanding your experiences. Your sense of humor allows you to enjoy life in a somewhat absurd way. You also know you will make mistakes and grow from these. You can be happy without feeling guilty when others are not as happy.

KEEPING THE GOLDEN RULE

Unfortunately, we may find it difficult to stay consistently happy with ourselves. Remember the Golden Rule: "Love your neighbor as you love yourself?" If we were to judge ourselves by this rule some of us haven"t been taking very good care of our neighbors. We have to be able to love and appreciate ourselves before we can do the same for others.

How do you love yourself? Sit down and give yourself a warm hug? Maybe, but probably not. Let's take a moment to consider who you are. On a sheet of paper, list 10 good attributes or characteristics about yourself. Examples might include intelligent, kind, giving, humorous and so on. Finish all 10 before reading on. We'll wait for you.

Did you write at least 10? Great, we knew a Motivator could do it. Go back and rank these from 10 to 1 with 10 representing the most important attribute in your opinion.

As you look back at these, how long have you felt this way about yourself for each one?

10.   5.

9.   4.

8.   3.

7.   2.

6.   1.

Look at the attribute you ranked as number 10, why is this a great attribute to have?

Without comparing yourself to others, what are your reasons for believing you are okay? List at least 5 reasons.

Look back at what you have written. Record how you feel? What kind of person are you?

Now on a separate sheet write a 40 word epitaph about who you are without including your achievements and accomplishments.

To reinforce that good opinion of yourself put the epitaph on your mirror or in your car to read every morning and night for the next 21 days or longer. Even if you feel you don't need to, do it as an experiment and measure how much better you feel after 21 days.

THE WORTH OF THE MOTIVATOR

Motivators are wonderful people, we come in all sizes..physical and mental with many different energy levels and senses of time urgency. We love to give to others because of the good we see occurring in them and the warm feelings of satisfaction we have in our hearts. We tend to live self actualized lives and want others to live close to their full potential as well because we know how good it feels. Work is a wonderfully positive expression of who we are and who we hope to become. We inspire, influence and motivate others through our words and our examples.

We create new thoughts that challenge others to new levels of existence. We challenge ourselves to new heights. We are good people who have much to do and much to give. Some of us allow ourselves less gratitude than we rightly deserve. The reasons for this are often due to other's influences over our behavior.

All too often, Motivators are beleaguered by the mocking jealous or envious ones who try to lead everyone to their level of mediocrity. We are told to be and do less by others who need to do more. We are unusual people with much personal growth behind and ahead of us. We need to live life at a pace that we internally know is right for us. The mockers truly pay us a compliment when they mock us. Their jealousy hurts them more than it does us. We must live our lives using our God given strengths, to do less is to be less than we rightfully should be and we deprive others of our gifts.

If we are 100 yard dashers, then we had better be quick and efficient in our race through a life time. If we are marathoners we need to mentally, emotionally and physically prepare ourselves for a full life of effort with appropriate amounts of rest. We need to train ourselves to enjoy every minute of our work without the need to justify to others our seemingly enormous capacity to do so. Others, unknowingly are envious and compare their achievements to ours and determine we should do less so they will feel worthwhile or so we will spend more time with them.

One Motivator explained the learning process in the following manner: "My parents and boyfriend were always complaining how I never spent enough time with them. I loved them but I grew more independent because of my resistance to their value projections on me. It took me a long time to realize I was OK and I enjoyed what I did and wanted to do more. The love relationship ended. My parents found other people and activities to make their lives richer without me. I found a new friend who encourages me to be me. I came to a new level of self appreciation and learned to ignore the world's dictates of being less so I can fit into the average mold. I am who I am and I'm loving it."

When we accept ourselves we are accepting our wants and desires, thus negating the pressures from others to be like them. Each Motivator is really an unique creation with special purposes and goals. To dissuade the Motivator from reaching his or her inspirational goals harms this person immeasurably. The internal pain of not meeting other's expectations even if they're negative can be draining. Some Motivators will choose to overtly ignore the statements similarly to the Motivator in the last paragraph. This too, is a mental drain.

On the other hand, accepting yourself and believing that your behavior is normal for you is a freeing event. One Motivator described it ..."When I realized that I was normal, I had a tremendous sensation of freedom and exhilaration. Other's 'shoulds' were no longer important. I love to think and work. I also enjoy playing because it makes me feel good. Physical exercise not only relaxes me but it stimulates me to consider life from another plane. I used to feel I had to concentrate on winning in tennis then I went through a stage of playing to enjoy the exertion. In another phase I would swim or cross country ski trying to ignore the philosophical thoughts that were crowding in my mind trying to just enjoy. Then it happened one day, I realized it was perfectly normal to live in my desires of the moment. I could choose to notice the moment's full intent or just enjoy the beauty of the moment. Whatever I wanted I could choose to do. I could enjoy sensory minutiae or broad life schemes without feeling the pressure of judgment. In Transactional Analysis language, my Child and Adult were free from the Parental rules. I had come home! I was astonished to find that home was within me waiting patiently with the warm smile of a self acceptance fire in the hearth. I was free..."

THE FREEDOM OF SELF ACCEPTANCE

Freeing yourself to be what you are is self acceptance. For the Motivator, one of Douglas McGregor's statements regarding Theory Y Management Assumptions is applicable, "work becomes as easy as play." Doing as much as you feel comfortable doing without physically harming yourself is the desire of the day. Each Motivator must come to terms with his or her physical, emotional and spiritual needs.

When work becomes a neurotic obsession with its goal to build self esteem or self acceptance, the person has become an unhealthy workaholic. This is not the style of a healthy Motivator. Unfortunately, Motivators have been confused with workaholics by the vast majority of their associates. This has grieved many Motivators and perhaps robbed them of their full capacity of self acceptance. It is a difficult task to explain that you are normal for you especially when others all around you think you are abnormal. They burned witches for being different, didn't they?

THE SECRETS OF SELF ACCEPTANCE

You have discovered the secret of self acceptance when you know it doesn't matter what others think of you. You are who you are and that's enough. Others will try to impose their rules upon your behavior. Yet you still have the right to be who you are without worrying or feeling guilty that you are not like the rest of the crowd. You are a Motivator with tremendous power to give and to enjoy life to its fullest measure. Only you can decide if you will be truly happy, being who you are or becoming what you want to be. Only you can know if you really love yourself. Others loving you helps but often it is not enough. Self acceptance is a continually unfolding process of learning new good and bad aspects of your character and relaxing with them. As we grow older, new values and weaknesses seem to pop up. Can you change and accept that you are not perfect? Your major traits become more ingrained and more visible. Will you be able to laugh at yourself and appreciate your idiosyncrasies even then? Hopefully so, because this is self acceptance too.

MOTIVATION BEGINS AT HOME

A leader is the foundation for a revved up group of motivated and enthusiastic employees. As a manager, supervisor or executive, you have a tremendous opportunity to be a leader by providing positive inputs to the working experiences of many lives. If you are a leader, you have the most important role on the team. Your employees will likely follow your lead. Usually if you are highly motivated and enthusiastic with them, they will respond in the same way. The results include increased productivity, efficiency, better quality and a pleasant working atmosphere. New ideas and creative endeavors freely develop in this kind of environment. People will be enthusiastic and excited about working on your team. Is there a manager or supervisor, who would prefer anything less?

Prior to motivating others, you need to tap the motivation within yourself. Many of us are mere shadows of what we can be. Our limited perceptions of who we are confines us. If you know who you are, what you can be and enjoy becoming as well as appreciating your current strengths then you have tapped into your motivation.

To realize this full potential, you need to appreciate yourself. Self acceptance must become deeply embedded in your bones. You are a valuable person to the people who know you. This value and worth is based upon who you are personally and is separate from your title and position. Recognizing and accepting your value in this manner increases your motivation. A high motivational level helps you to be productive and effective in your position.

Self acceptance starts at home. Once you accept yourself, you are more likely to accept others. Your impact will be far greater if you have the ability to accept not only other's failings but your own as well. If you're not positive with your own life, then you can't be positive about others. When you are a positive individual, then you are able to give more to those who need your perspective and wisdom to develop their own potential.

Take a few moments now to write in the space below your strengths that contribute to you being or becoming a fine manager/supervisor.

Now, list below all the good parts of your life and your work. In other words, what can you appreciate in your life and work?

Each day, pull out this list and review it. Add to it each day. These are things to be grateful for.

Remember you're OK, in fact, you're terrific. How long has it been since you looked in a mirror and decided to give yourself compliments? Do it today. Say aloud something like "I am great. I'm a good person. I have many admirable traits. I feel good. I am good." Make up your own statements and say them to yourself while looking in the mirror.

DUSTING OFF YOUR SELF IMAGE

In order to give the utmost to others, your self image has to be well nourished. It is a basic principle that many forget to apply. You need to see the good within yourself first in order to perceive and securely help others. Otherwise, you operate on zero and hurt yourself by giving out. If you are able to see and believe your own potential, you can become a healthy Motivator.

To unlock the Motivator power in you means unlocking your own sense of self esteem. You can do this by recognizing you are a unique individual and the world would not be a better place without you. We recall a Christmas movie several years ago in which a young woman despaired and wished she had never been born. Fortunately, an angel showed her what life without her would have meant. Many people would have not been touched by her goodness. The lack of this single solitary life meant death for one man, alcoholism for another and jail for another.

In reviewing your own life, ask yourself, who have you helped along the way? How have you made someone's life more rewarding? Don't be modest. Undoubtedly, you've helped someone or possibly many people. Have you ever said a kind word to someone who seemed depressed? Have you helped a friend or neighbor in a time of need? Or have you helped them build or fix something? Have you stopped to help a stranded motorist? Have you talked and listened to a young person who needed advice?

In fact, listening is one of the greatest compliments a person can give another. One Motivator, who doesn't know she's a Motivator is one of the authors' mother. She encouraged the author to keep going during some rough growing spots in college. She listened to her daughter's dreams and even said she believed in them. She listened to the frustrations and tribulations of starting a business. Most of all she gave her unrequited love throughout the years as a parent. That is being an extraordinary Motivator. A listening person is unusual but a listening Motivator is even more exceptional. Perhaps you too, have helped someone by listening.

ACCEPTING THE CHALLENGE

Are you ready to unlock the Motivator within you? We believe that if you want to become a Motivator, having read how wonderful Motivators are, and are willing to accept the risk of becoming a Work Addict, you can be a Motivator or already are one. You may be among the many who have never considered themselves Motivators but in actuality have a tremendous effect on many lives. We have isolated numerous characteristics of Motivators but none is as important as having a mission of motivating, giving, inspiring or just plain helping others. Motivators' achievements are measurable in changes in people's lives and in their results. Motivators get a terrific charge from helping people develop their talents.

On a nonverbal level, if you can communicate empathically and unlock something magical in other people, you are or are becoming a Motivator. Being action oriented is essential. Motivators move and go forward 80% of the time at full speed. To do this you need a strong inner drive. Are you a go getter or do you want to do more? Even if you don't think of yourself as a go getter, if you want to do more, help others, and achieve more, you have the power to motivate.

DO YOU CHOOSE THE MISSION OR DOES IT CHOOSE YOU?

One Motivator said her mission was both a personal decision and one of having been chosen. As she described it:

"Back in the early 50's I was intrigued by Sputnik and then our space program. I decided at age 5 that I would become an astronomer and help people by discovering something that would make the world a better place. I also wanted to be famous. So I began to read books, some of which I couldn't understand. I memorized facts about the stars and our solar system. I held on to that goal even though it meant enduring some social pressure from my family for seeming to be a little weird. I was always asking myself questions about how certain machines worked. My great desire was to create an anti-gravity machine so I could fly.

Well, I held on to that mission of becoming an Astronomer until a month before I started college. It was at that time that I realized I wasn't too happy, something was bothering me. I contacted a friend who had helped me become a Christian several years before. She suggested that I tell God that He could direct my life. Well, I didn't want to do that because I had a sneaking suspicion that God did not want me to become an astronomer. She suggested that I ask Him to change my attitude if I wasn't suppose to be one. So after several hours of consideration while in the grass along a river bank on a sunny day, I decided to commit my life's work to His purpose.

Well, two months later I discovered astronomers need to understand chemistry. Unfortunately, chemistry was always a leap of faith for me. I found if I chose the answer that I thought was wrong on the test that it was the right answer. Chemistry, unlike math and physics never seemed to make sense to me. So I decided to change my major. I chose to take journalism and communications classes later that year. I decided I should become a journalist because I enjoyed writing. However, I asked God to stop me in some way if I wasn't supposed to become a journalism major. The very day I was heading out to change my major field of study, a young man who had been in both classes with me asked me.where I was going. I told him I was changing my my major to a journalism major. He told me I should become a communications major for various reasons. So since I had decided that if someone stopped me that meant God had other plans for me. . .I went into communicaitons which was the best decision for my life's work: being a consultant. So, in a sense, I chose the first mission and the second mission chose me. I have also claimed an old Biblical statement in which God says 'I know the plans I have for you, plans for welfare and not for calamity but to give you a future and a hope.' I have believed that statement is a personal contract that I have with God. My career has been built on those few words. The result of that belief in my mission has given me not only financial rewards but good feelings of accomplishment."

Another Motivator described a feeling of excitement when she discovered her mission. One question is to ask yourself "What really excites you and what do you enjoy doing?"

The mission is a basic ingredient for realizing your power to motivate. If you can determine your purpose, you can become a Motivator. Those who are not motivated seem dull to Motivators because that means a lack of excitement. Work and life is exciting to Motivators. Life becomes an integrated whole of hobbies, work, love and passion. Some Motivators have the mission to turn people into Motivators so they can enjoy life to the fullest. This desire is very similar to a religious zeal. Motivators want people to become more than what they are, which is to reach their full potential.

DISCOVERING THE GRAND PLAN FOR THEIR LIVES

His or her mission may lay dormant for a number of years, then something triggers the response and a Motivator is born. One Motivator conjectured, "Although I think you're born with it, I also think you can develop it. Many people are given this inherent talent by their parents."

Consider: Did you feel you could motivate people from early on?

Did you feel somewhat alienated as a young person because there was something different about you?

Were you planning your career at an early age? Did you think of yourself as a leader?

Did someone early in your life reinforce that it was okay to be different or unique?

Motivators typically have a very strong opinions of how they should be and sometimes how others should be. They have weathered the early storms of pressures in life to develop a strong sense of rightness for their behavior.

For others, early role models showed them how to be and do. The principles taught are still models of behavior for today.

THOSE WHO COULD BE MOTIVATORS

For those who aren't Motivators, something seems to stand in their way of accepting a mission. Often the greatest of these is fear. The common fears expressed are...

> * what if I don't like it
> * what if I make an error in judgment

* what if I fail
* what if I succeed

Other reasons include they are unsure of what they want or they haven't had many successes to gage what they are good at doing. The saddest is when a person has such a low sense of self esteem that he or she doesn't see the great potential within.

FINAL NOTES ON REALIZING YOUR POWER

To realize your hidden power to motivate, you can learn by being or doing what we have suggested. Yet becoming a Motivator is more of a matter of desire than a step by step process. Desiring to be one will help you become one. Our philosophy is that motivation is energy waiting to be released or turned on. You can turn on that power for yourself by desiring to help yourself and others.

C-2 DEVELOPING THE PRODUCTIVE MOTIVATED TEAM

DEVELOPING THE PRODUCTIVE TEAM

Are you excited about being a Motivator? Great! Now we want to show you how to turn that energy into being a manager who motivates. Using the motivation power you have in your possession is a key component of producing a productive team.

There are two steps to developing a more productive team. You have already taken the first step by examining your own strengths. Be pleased and grateful for who you are. The second step is a extension of the first. Think about the value of your employees--to you and the team. Then communicate that value to them. By counting your work place blessings, the result is a more positive outlook and you have greater potential to succeed.

The UNDERLYING PRINCIPLE IS if you give in a positive manner to your employees, they will give positive results to you.

From our seminars, we have found that managers who apply this principle achieve amazing results with their employees.

What kind of image do you project to your team? Are you projecting that they are valuable assets or that they can be easily replaced. A major share of what you project, depends upon your self esteem and your attitudes about your team. If you communicate positive attitudes, the results will bear the fruits of these thoughts. The converse is also true. If you perceive your employees as just a necessary evil or that they are not valuable, you will probably have a working group who grudgingly gives in return.

As a manager, you have people to help you. Concentrate upon this aspect rather than concentrating on a perception that people are not working up to their full potential. Concentrate on what they are giving and on their strengths. Everyone has at least one strength. Look for it. Think about it. Focus on it!

A. Think about each employee who reports to you. What strengths do you see in each one? Write these down. Try to generate at least 5 for each person.

B. Then think about them. How does it make you feel to have such talented people working with you?

C. What will you say to each person that acknowledges the preceding awareness? When will you do it?

DEVELOPING A MOTIVATED TEAM

Plan a motivational strategy. How can you effectively motivate your people?

On the corporate level, a conscious effort should be made to develop the teams. Team approaches can create a motivated work force. When a team works together to get a big contract, every member counts. Every member deserves to hear and enjoy the success of getting the contract. People are typically motivated by knowing how "their" roles helped put the contract over the goal line and why they are important to the team. The team concept is a "WE" concept with the leader setting the pace for the team. The manager is the leader of the team. It is expressed in this manner: "we're going to do this together." It may mean we've got special tasks and ordinary tasks to do together. The key is we are doing it as a team, as a unit that cares about its members. Each member's contribution is valuable to the team's efforts.

A conscientious effort needs to be made in forming and developing a team. This means determining common goals for the team. Letting people know what part they play in achieving these goals. Proper emphasis must also be placed upon the results of achieving the predetermined goals. Within corporations, emphasis should be placed upon how individual goals and corporate goals can work together. Employee participation is an essential element of team building. Employee participation means asking and listening to what your employees say when you ask their opinions.

It is demotivational when managers don't listen to employee ideas or if they down grade ideas on the spot without taking time and effort to consider them.

The roles on the team are important to emphasize to your players. You will want to carefully identify why and what their roles contribute and how their roles interrelate. In the sports world, each player knows how his/her role impacts upon the rest of the team's performance. In the organizational world, this is also appropriate. It's essential to define what each player's piece of the action is in meeting the group's goals.

If the organization is in flux or moving through structural change, often the middle management team becomes confused about the company's expectations for them. With resources being shifted or reduced, some middle managers of one huge manufacturing company found they were having trouble meeting new goals and responsibilities that hadn't been clearly defined but had instead been dumped upon them. In addition, laws regarding treatment of employees and working with the unions have complicated the communication role they must exercise.

Many managers express frustration with finding their old management styles are no longer welcome and ineffective. The way to be a good manager has changed because people have changed. People want to be a part of the decision making rather than a part of the adversarial team when working with management. Even unions are changing some because they see the need to change if they are to survive automation. Employees are from different generations and have different cultural expectations. The old ways to motivate have given way to newer methods.

There are many different management styles that can be effective with different types of people. As always it's the matching of the appropriate style with the needs of the people. Some are more effective than others. There is no one most effective style.

CREATING THE MOTIVATIONAL CLIMATE

Ruth Martens, an executive with the American Cancer Society, commented about this area: "A manager creates a climate conducive to motivation by being positive, enthusiastic, developing good listening skills and by demonstrating a willingness to reward for effort. I think reward for effort is a key. Maybe not for winning but certainly for effort and winning too, of course."

People are your assets as a manager to develop. If you develop these assets properly, they will expand their capabilities. They must be protected and sustained as well. If you overwork them and forget to laugh with them, they will be laughing at you as they walk out the door to new jobs. Simple? Yet all too often, managers forget working effectively with people is different from working with schedules, plans, paper work and figures. Good people are not a replenishable source. If you are stingy with pay and praise, you are the one to pay the bill in the long run. Your people will not support you when you need them most.

The converse is also true, good people are attracted to excellent managers. An excellent manager knows what motivates his or her people. This motivation is freely given and will create appropriate performance. People will work hard for you if they know you care about them and show you care by substantial actions.

A COMPANY'S GREATEST RESOURCES ARE ITS PEOPLE

One engineer was quite irate about the consultants assisting his company with engineering problems, they were having. He resented that the consultants would talk to the people on the production line about what was wrong and then tell management what they, themselves, could have easily determined if they had taken the time to listen. He felt the consultants should be able to be brilliant enough to solve the problems on their own. He was overlooking a critical point - that management was either unwilling or not aware that the answers were as close as their own people.

People Wealth. A COMPANY'S GREATEST RESOURCES ARE ITS PEOPLE. If you deny this fact it will hinder you from becoming the best. The best managers are those who understand and use this fact to their advantage. The worst managers are those who exploit their people. Over the long haul, they will not survive, nor will their companies.

One example has occurred numerous times throughout the history of companies. A new employee sees a problem, develops a solution and presents it to management. Management's common reply prior to listening fully..."we tried that and it didn't work." If a person had a nickel for every time that had been said in the last five years, they would be very wealthy.

The BRILLIANT MANAGER, WHO knows how to motivate people, listens and truly considers the solution. He or she may even say "let's give it a try." Just because a solution didn't work in the past doesn't mean it won't work this time. Management has the responsibility to listen and actively solicit the trust of their people. When people trust the manager or supervisor, anything is possible. Many managers recognize this intellectually but don't practice it. These same managers believe they are good listeners and communicators, they will say as much in our seminars. Many are but many are in error. If you were to ask their people, you would find they are busy people but people who don't give enough to their employees in terms of asking questions and really listening.

The concerned manager spends more time with people than with paper. We challenge every manager or supervisor reading this book to take a very brave step and to ask your people if they think you spend enough time with them listening to their problems and concerns. When you ask them, ask them to write it anonymously and return it to you. Based upon their responses, change your behavior somewhat. Realize that we can all become better managers and supervisors. If they write something negative, see it as an opportunity for you to improve and for them to vent some frustrations. If you get no criticism, truly examine your behavior and ask yourself if there's still a way you could improve.

There is so much potential that remains untapped out there. It's like the miner who was digging for gold in South Africa and overlooked the diamonds in the dirt all around him. Every executive, entrepreneur, manager, and supervisor has a tremendous amount of wealth in the employees. Corporate America's greatest exigence is to know the inner secrets of how to make people feel good greatest exigence is to know the inner secrets of how to make people feel good about themselves and their work. It's really quite easy once you've learned it, yet until you have mastered it, it is another story.

TEN ESSENTIAL MOTIVATION STRATEGIES

The question, you're probably asking is "How can I get them motivated?" Here are ten essential strategies to accomplish that objective. As an executive, entrepreneur, manager, or supervisor, these can help you develop the productive motivated team. The best managers have learned these ten strategies and use them frequently.

1. GET YOUR OWN ACT TOGETHER.

Manage your own life well before you start to manage others' lives. We've noted this strategy in the last chapter, but it is essential to motivation, and therefore worth repeating.

The manager who sees himself or herself as a Motivator has an edge on this game of worker motivation. Ask yourself as a manager/supervisor, what are you excited about regarding your work? What do you enjoy most about your job? Looking back on why you were chosen for the position, you must have some strengths. What are those strengths? Concentrate on those for a moment. Brag a bit to yourself about those. Concentrate on those braggings. What is positive about what you're doing? Why is it of a positive nature? What can you get excited about? How can you communicate your excitement to your employees?

If you as an executive, entrepreneur, manager, or supervisor are excited about your work, then your people will become excited about their work. Excitement is very contagious. With a team of highly enthusiastic and motivated people, you have a tremendously productive team of people. They will be able to handle needs and problems, you would never see from your view point.

Jane Rhodes, Director of Buildings and Facilities for the State of Michigan told us her perspective regarding enthusiasm, "Enthusiasm is the key to motivation. . .if you're excited about something, you tend to motivate others to be excited about whatever you're high in the sky about." We agree enthusiasm is an intangible that can be given and received. In order to communicate your enthusiasm, you have to have it and be willing to share it in such a way that others eagerly want to join in.

Enthusiasm is a visible result of getting your act together. When you know who you are and like yourself you tend to manage your life and others better. Coming to like yourself is a life long continuous upward moving process. Each new level reached is a point of discovery of loving your good aspects and understanding your weaknesses.

2. HELP YOUR TEAM MEMBERS FEEL GOOD ABOUT THEMSELVES.

This means allowing them to fully realize their dignity and personal value. Your positive comments will help improve their self esteem. Your actions will also support their levels of self acceptance.

An executive who manages numerous people gave his philosophy regarding motivation and helping employees to value themselves. "Everyone is motivated. By their very nature, everybody is inquisitive, aggressive and wanting to accomplish things....The only time that people become unmotivated is when they start assimilating someone else's attitude into their essence....The main thing that you have to do if you're going to motivate someone is to get them to believe in themselves. Believe that it's possible....When I go into somebody's life I have an innate belief that they can do it. Just general belief in someone being able to accomplish something will more than motivate them. There's the honest to God concern and 'I know you can do it, Charlie, if you want to go do it, do it.' That puts a challenge in front of a human being that can't be resisted because then you challenge their inner core. You don't put a carrot in front of them, you don't kick them in the butt, you get inside their soul and all of a sudden they have to admit to themselves 'I am worthy of doing that.'"

Another Motivator has observed a similar phenomenon..."I heard several people say..'if it weren't for so and so, I wouldn't be where I am and I would have left the company a long time ago.' The idea was 'somebody took a chance on me, somebody believed more for me than I could believe for myself and I will not let them down.'"

Employees who feel good about themselves often want to fully use their abilities. To assist your employees discover ways of doing this, you might want to consider the advice of one of the Motivators we interviewed: "Find out what that individual wants. Include your own perception about the potential that you see in that person and offer them the opportunities to achieve it and then let the person determine whether or not they want to reach their potential, because I think that's a choice for everybody. If a person doesn't want to reach it, I don't care how hard you work, they'll not do it. Until somebody believes in something and selects that as their own philosophy you can offer them the moon and they'll not take it if they don't believe in it."

Another method of helping them feel good about themselves was presented to us by Olga Holden, Director of Human Resources and Planning of the John Henry Company, "You have to absolutely hand over some of the credit to the people. If somebody has worked on a project...even at the risk of violating protocol..they will go with me to present the thing. I have never lost any of the lime light by doing that. I feel so strongly about it. I tell people they've done it and I give them the credit." We have seen Olga do this in several management positions and it is a very effective means of not only motivating but elevating the credibility of the people she gives credit to. Further, she garners a tremendous amount of respect and loyalty from her people by this and other effective management methods.

3. MOTIVATE BY GETTING THEM INTERESTED IN THE VALUE OF WHO THEY ARE AND WHAT THEY DO.

Every job and every task has value. In this society we have placed too much or too little value on tasks, without regard to motivation or the self esteem of people. For too long in this century, we have isolated some jobs into the never never land of "I'd never want to do that!" If people are to be motivated they must feel worthy of their tasks. Every job has value to the organization or to society. When management gives time to establishing value in the job of their employees, employees can gain a sense of self esteem from the successful accomplishment of their work.

Another way to show you believe they have value is to respect their ideas. Everyone who knows they are important gets respect from others. Your employees will be motivated if they know their ideas are important to you especially if you seek them. Write their ideas down. That shows you really want to use their ideas. It's also worthwhile to capture their ideas on paper so you don't forget them.

We've heard so much about team building, what does it all mean? Building a team means building up individuals. We have said that each person needs to be able to see his or her role very clearly and know importance is placed upon that role. One manager had a rather unique way of emphasizing this to his people. When a particularly difficult project was given to his team. He introduced the project by showing slides of each of his team members while playing the music from the "Mission Impossible" television show at the staff meeting. He announced their individual specialty in a very strictly defined method. Needless to say these people felt special. Hokey? No, these people felt it was a creative way to say he knew they could do it, that he appreciated their efforts and he saw the high value of those individual efforts.

Another way is this expression one manager used by saying "Without you doing this job we couldn't succeed. You're an essential part of this team." One key question to ask yourself is "How would I feel if someone told me I was great or essential?" Every job is important. Those who enjoy their jobs see the work as important or worth doing well. People often need to see the significance of the job related to themselves and/or to society. People want to feel that they are worthwhile. You can realize your power to motivate by helping them to feel worthwhile during an activity that requires the majority of their life: work.

Every job is important or the person wouldn't be a part of the organization. One Motivator told us that he felt "managers and supervisors have to be involved with their employees to sit down and hash out problems to find out when there's a problem." The concerns of the employees become the concerns of the manager. People need to feel their needs are being considered and that they are important. No one wants to feel like their job isn't very important when they spend at least 40 hours per week and many ancillary hours in preparation for work. The manager who has learned to communicate to each person that their job is worthwhile and thus the person is worthwhile, has learned a vital secret to keeping a motivated worker. The manager must be sincere in his or her statements about the job's importance. If you have difficulty doing this, think about what it would be like if this person's position didn't exist, who would do the work?

One person that is often overlooked or belittled is the secretary. Secretaries need to hear not only if they did a good job but what was the result of their part of the work. Was the proposal accepted? Was the report approved? Did you go back and say to your secretary something like "getting this proposal done and out in a timely fashion gave us an edge on the competition, thank you for your hard work." Even if you don't succeed, it's important to tell them that and say something like: "we didn't make it this time but we really appreciate your effort." Every person who has had a part in working on a special project should hear the result of their work, whether the project succeeds or fails.

4. LEAD BY EXAMPLE. SHOW THEM WHAT IT MEANS TO BE MOTIVATED.

Another Motivator stated that "corporate leadership from the CEO on down needs to be motivated and believe in what they are doing. They must model their motivation and enthusiasm for their people."

We have noted that to motivate others as an executive, entrepreneurs, manager, or supervisor, you need to be motivated yourself. Certainly, we've suggested several strategies in other sections of the book. However, we think particular attention should be given to the manager. We have noted throughout our many years of working with executives, entrepreneur, managers and supervisors that management is a rough job. The short cuts usually don't work.

Management is a relationship between a group of people and one individual. This individual has to plan, rule, control, motivate, communicate, listen and be willing to work long hours. Sometimes this individual inherits a team of unmotivated individuals, who like to play unhealthy games with each other and the boss.

The three most important roles to creating a productive and motivated team are the Leader, Motivator Manager and Communicator. The Leader projects the examples by action as well as through language and delegated authority. Knowing what motivates his or her employees as well as himself or herself and behaving in accordance with this knowledge, are the first steps to being a Motivator Manager. The Communicator role is essential to both being a Leader and a Motivator. As an effective Communicator, the manager can effectively motivate others to perform good work for the organization. If any of these skills is deficient, the productivity suffers and thus profits or services are less than they could be.

Over the years, we have observed a direct relationship between the manager's motivational level and the motivational level of the employees reporting to that manager. Managers who are highly motivated, communicate their enthusiasm and expect enthusiasm of their employees, tend to generate enthusiasm in their employees. These elements are essential to the equation.

We've noticed managers who are motivated but forget or neglect to communicate this enthusiasm to their employees. Sometimes managers communicate, but in glowing four letter expletives. Either of these cases can be an employee Demotivator. Who wants to give their all to something the boss isn't really interested in? Others forget to tell their employees what they expect from them regarding quality, enthusiasm, timeliness and the rewards of good performance. The most respected managers communicate their own motivation and enthusiasm as well as their expectations to their employees every day.

John Green, an business consultant and manager commented that "You want to give a person something they can do and immediately win with. Then acknowledge the job for having been done. Not necessarily raving about it but simply acknowledging it did get done. I think the greatest sin committed by managers today is they fail to acknowledge a person completed the project. So the person never got a sense of reward for having completed the project. So there's no payoff for completing projects, then."

We fully recognize that there are times when it's really hard to be the leader of the group. The problem occurs when you stop leading and continue to just be. If you don't show a motivated example, your team will not be able to surpass you in motivational level. There are days when you may not feel very motivated. Sometimes it's easier to just be. On those days, you have options. You can choose to hibernate in your office and try to hide the blah feeling. You can also choose to create a positive self attitude; "I will look and act highly motivated today for my people because they deserve it. I will think positive thoughts and discipline myself to think of something else when I think about how bad I feel." Attitudes can be changed.

It's a tough road to walk when you're in a supervisory or management position. Ask yourself, "what do my people need to see and hear from me today? Do they want an enthusiastic, optimistic manager/supervisor or a tired, worn, pessimistic manager/supervisor?" Remember your strengths, you can reach into yourself and come out a winner. Remember you set the pace. What kind of pace do you want to set?

If you want your employees to be motivated, demonstrate energy and motivation by your behavior. Talk slightly faster in an excited pace and tone about a special aspect of work. Your posture and nonverbal signals should signify life, energy, enthusiasm and a certain sense of pride. A motivated person usually walks faster, smiles more, makes eye contact and has eyes that sparkle. These physical clues are external symbols of what is really going on inside. People can't help but catch your enthusiasm.

Another motivational hint is used by Pam Czuj, Executive Director, Personal Dynamics Center: "I think it's important to be sure that you don't forget the play aspect. Be humorous. Let the good feelings that you have about what you're doing show. It's going to rub off....it will be infectious. Whenever possible approach things with humor. This 'deadly serious, all work and no play' is ridiculous in any organization." We agree. Work should be fun.

5. BE A LEADER AND A WORKING TEAM MEMBER.

This concept has been used before and should continue. The team works together to get the high score. Many people are motivated by working together to reach a common good. We have only to look at the history around World War II to see how people can work together to achieve great goals. Today, manufacturing companies such as General Motors, Ford and Chrysler are changing their strategies of where teams can be effective. Hourly workers are forming teams with their supervisors to work on problems. The Japanese have been doing it for years. Research has shown the best decisions and strategies evolve from teams of people, not just one super individual. Two miraculous Motivators occur: 1) commitment to the strategy and 2) enthusiasm to make a process work.

The manager or supervisor must be a part of this team otherwise many benefits of the process are lost. Many times the manager is not considered a part of the team. The manager gives orders but forgets to become a part of the team work. To be a part of the team, you need to demonstrate the "we-ness" otherwise you're perceived as a outsider who is manipulating. As the manager or supervisor, you're the leader of the team or the coach.

This situation of leaderless teams has probably evolved as warfare has evolved. In ancient times, the leader was in front leading the charge. In modern warfare, the leader is behind the lines strategizing. Certain key military figures have overcome this by visiting the troops or giving rousing speeches before a key battle.

Somehow, this has spread to some companies. The manager briefly puts on his/her leader helmet to put the team into action and then disappears until after the battle. Now if you have a team that would prefer you were resting on the sidelines then, by all means stay out of the way. However, be sure you're available for giving advice. As a Motivator, you're going to want to be in the thick of things to encourage and do your part of the impossible task.

We remember the manager of a dietetics department in a hospital, who described team play as similar in nature to buying a train ticket. After you buy the ticket (employment), you either get on the train or stand and watch it go by. His employees loved this analogy and continued with various aspects of trains and working for the railroad. They saw it as a means of describing their work together. With this and many other team building strategies, his team has flourished.

6. LISTEN TO YOUR PEOPLE.

A sales manager aptly stated a variation of this concept for us, "One has to have empathy for the other individual...a great amount of empathy...the ability to walk in the other fellow's moccasins. Once you have empathy, I think it's a matter of developing your listening skills. Listening is very important in it's a matter of developing your listening skills. Listening is very important in motivating because its going to give you those clues as to what you need to do to find that so called hot button in the individual, ie., what motivates the individual."

Thorough listening means planning and taking time to ask questions of your employees in formal and informal settings. Often listening is required when they need it not when you need it. If you can't take the time when they are requesting it, set another time to do it. Don't say "I'll get back to you" and then forget it. Set a specific time on your calendar with enough time to deal with the issue.

Key idea: Set an appointment with employees. We do with clients and others outside the organization, our employees need to feel that specialness of having special and regular appointments with us. It becomes a protected time from other conflicts and interruptions, thus becoming quality time. Make it time with the doors closed and have your phone answered by someone else. The first few times, the employees may be a little tense. Try to remember to tell them prior to the meeting that you're interested in hearing about their concerns to allay any fears they may have.

Ask your employees questions like these:

* *What do you enjoy most about your work?*
* *How would you like to change your work?*
* *What would help you do an even more effective job?*
* *What frustrates you the most about working here?*
* *What are your current problems at work?*
* *What improvements could we make in your work environment?*
* *What kind of work would you like to be doing in the next 8 months?*
* *What motivates you?*
* *Why do you work here?*
* *Why do you enjoy working?*
* *What are you working on now?*
* *Which projects do you find most interesting?*
* *Which do you find most challenging?*
* *What kinds of resources are you having trouble finding or locating?*
* *What do you need from me?*
* *What advice can I give you?*
* *What areas would you like suggestions in? Do you need suggestions?*
* *What's been your greatest satisfaction this week?*
* *What did you score best in this week?*
* *Which activity or accomplishment from this week are you proudest of?*
* *How could I help you further develop your talents and abilities?*
* *What would you like to learn more about?*
* *What skills would you like to develop?*

Although you wouldn't want to ask more than one of these types of questions at a time, a question like this or rephrased might supply you with some exciting information about your employee's motivational health. The employee may not be able to answer the question at first but it gets him/her thinking. It's very sincere desire to know.

This is an excellent Thursday or Friday morning activity for a 30 minute meeting with each employee. Make a standing appointment with each one. You can use several of these questions and make up some of your own. The essential element in this activity is that it centers around positive growth and is rewarding the employee's achievements with time.

It helps if you can do this in a conference room with only a note pad for notes. Environmental distractors should be blocked from attending your meeting.

After asking each question pause to allow them to think about the question. Smile and wait for a whole 60 seconds and you will be rewarded with their response. For those of you who get nervous waiting and want to fill the gap, silently count to 60. When they are speaking, take mental notes and record key statements. Concentrate on what they are saying. What is it they are saying verbally and nonverbally? What are they saying emotionally? What are they asking for psychologically? What else would you like to know about what they are talking about. Afterwards, take a few moments to think about the conversation from these viewpoints.

Ruth Martens of the American Cancer Society aptly stated her opinion about listening: "in order to motivate people you have to listen to what they are saying to you. You have to also perceive what they are saying to you through their body language. Motivators are good listeners to verbal and nonverbal language."

We suggest watching a good communicator, how do they communicate verbally, nonverbally and psychologically. Watch how they use touching, gestures, smiles and head nods to let people know they understand. Sometimes it's OK to touch an employee, on an appropriate spot. Sometimes it isn't.

Jackie Lichty, a sales executive stated her opinion about listening..."To me, listening is loving and I think that is ultimately what all of us want...to be loved. I think that the only way we can really do that is to listen to one another. So that the act of listening to another person talk is in fact exactly what it takes to motivate."

7. REESTABLISH THE LINK BETWEEN PAY AND PERFORMANCE.

Pay is no longer a motivator for many employees because they are unable to see the connection between working and payment for that value of work. For anyone who doesn't believe there's a direct relationship, they have to look no farther than the last recession. Companies had lost a significant portion of the market and workers lost wages and jobs. Typically, companies do not pay for people they don't need. Workers need to be motivated to see the link between working effectively and helping the companies solve problems rather than using the union to fight the companies. We have lost the psychological between working effectively and helping the companies solve problems rather than using the union to fight the companies. We have lost the psychological value of what money is and can be for workers. Money can be a motivator if it is linked to psychological benefits and as a reward for good work. "Security" in the form of a secure job has become a falsehood. No one truly has a secure job. Even large companies can suffer great losses or bankruptcy, therefore no job is 100% secure.

It's also important to let them know that getting a pay check is dependent upon the work that comes into the company. The work that is ordered is dependent upon their efforts in the areas of quality, productivity and service. No matter how big the organization is, their pay checks are interlinked with the product's purchase which is linked to customer satisfaction with quality and service. As a manager or supervisor you play an integral role in assuring that this is common knowledge and used every day.

As Motivators, managers need to give employees what they want. Surprisingly their wants are quite simple. People want to work where it's clean, safe and friendly. They want to accomplish their work and enjoy themselves. They want to be respected and feel trusted. They want to be paid fairly and to get bonuses or pay increases that are linked to performance rather than across the board cost of living increases.

Several companies such as Domino's Pizza give several bonuses per year rather than just one per year. One manufacturing company in Wisconsin gives a bonus to each employee every month based upon performance. This relates again to connecting pay with performance.

Many workers forget that the pay check and the work are directly related. Rather than wait for the next recession to reveal this, managers have a tremendous opportunity to create this integral link in the minds of their employees.

If you're a manager, a great way to reunite the concept of pay with performance is to deliver the pay checks to your employees, who report directly to you.

As you give them their checks, you have a wonderful opportunity to say "Thank you. I really appreciate your work on such and such." Sound strange? If you do this you'll see your employees may be a bit uncomfortable at first but keep it up and you'll have restored a significant part of work that has been lost to neglect. The subtleties create that underlying psychological impact of "you're worth every bit that we pay you"

In a sense we are completing an old fashion idea of the work triangle with the worker, work and the manager at each corner united to attain the many payoffs including pay, goals, satisfaction, pride and satisfied customers/public.

Give them feedback. You can make your employees' day by telling them that you appreciate their efforts and that they have value and worth. The many informal polls we've taken with employees, show that the most effective managers are the ones who express gratitude and appreciation through a few simple words such as, "Thank you. You did an excellent job on. . ." If you can't remember when you last said "Thank you," do it today and watch the magical results. Be sure to do it individually as well as in groups. Another part of the Motivator's description is to give employees a Psychic Pay Check each week. Many supervisors are concerned that they can't give their employees a raise or certain perks. Pure recognition of performance is a type of psychic pay check. Public recognition or recognizing their efforts in front of your boss easily promotes positive feelings within the employees. For example, you might say "This is what our team did and John/Julie played an essential role in that effort. He/she gave us a tremendous boost with his/her ideas at some key points."

Recognition can be given on the basis of whether the employees did the best job not whether they came in first. You can decide that first place can be awarded to those who try hard, not only to those who get the brass ring first.

8. RECOGNIZE EVERYONE IS BASICALLY WILLING TO DO A GOOD JOB.

Many excellent managers have said this to us over the years. Their recognition that people want to work has been well supported by their employee's efforts. Those who believed the opposite, that they have lazy employees have seen the results of their beliefs...poor workmanship, absenteeism, and for some the failure of their businesses.

Another sales manager described her beliefs regarding this strategy: "I think basically people want to do a good job. They will do that themselves without anybody else motivating them to do that. I think everybody wants to do a good job. If they have the tools to do that, the training and whatever else is needed, most people will be their own police officer. I think everybody's police officer has a different size club that he carries around. Some people really need a lot of pats on the back and they literally will not do a whole lot unless they are continually reinforced. There are other people that if you don't talk to them for six months that's great with them. You have to be real sensitive to the different personalities and try to second guess or come right out and ask them: "What do you need?"

In organizations, we usually have a multi-ethnic-racial-religious-gender work force to motivate and communicate with. Old motivation techniques might not be as effective today. Consider your methods, have you been getting the results you are seeking? What are your methods? Do you vary these methods with people. Do you know what motivates each of your employees?

9. BE A POSITIVE PYGMALION

Many times the manager can be a positive Pygmalion for an employee. As a Motivator manager, you can ignite the spark of an employee's potential capabilities. Many successful people take time each day to visualize their own goals and desires. This same principle can be applied to managing others. Think about your employees' strengths. What can you do today to help them realize more of these potentials?

As one manager described this strategy, "Sometimes I say to a person, 'You have a tremendous talent and great potential. I'd like to be able to offer you an opportunity to achieve some things that you might not even think are apparent right now. I would like to give you an opportunity to do that because I have seen certain qualities in you. I don't know how you feel about that and I don't know if that would be something that you'd like to do. If you are willing to work toward it, I can't guarantee you that you will get a certain thing but I can tell you that you'll build and develop the qualities that will help you achieve something in terms of the institution. You'll be able to increase your stature and you'll be more productive.'"

Belief is a powerful motivational strategy that you can use with your employees and yourself. Many songs in the last twenty years have expressed the results and power of believing in yourself. Jane Rhodes told us how she uses the song "Believe In Yourself" from the movie "The Wiz." "I turn the volume up so that it shakes the wall of my brick house. If you believe in yourself then there is nothing anyone else can do to challenge you, to put you down or to make you fail." Music stimulates people to new levels of the excitement and determination to achieve. It seems to allow people to overlook their frailties and to believe in their hidden strengths. It can serve as positive Pygmalion for yourself and for your employees.

As a manager, being a positive Pygmalion by believing in your employees is one of the greatest gifts you can give them, your company and yourself. By stating your belief in them, they know they can count on you to be an encouraging factor in their growth and skill development. Most people need to hear such encouraging words.

Think about your employees, who needs to hear that you believe he or she can accomplish some new or more expansive job? Perhaps today would be a good day to tell him or her.

10. ACTIVELY TRUST THEM

The nature of work has changed, so has the role of manager as a monitor. That's passe. Today's role is one of the MOTIVATOR. Belief in their potential is a key ingredient of this. To the extent that you trust people, they will prove that trust back a hundred fold.

Note what this manager told us about his relationship with his people: "In my department, I have given my people complete responsibility and that's ok because I have trained them so I trust in what they're doing. In addition they get a percentage of the profits of the department. They are frankly the most dedicated people in the department. Letting people earn a little bit more than they're worth everyday to a degree fosters all kinds of loyalties."

One of the questions we have asked managers and supervisors is "Think of the best manager you've worked for, what actions, behaviors and what things did they say that made them effective?" We find the best managers know how to communicate appreciation, respect and trust for the employees' ideas and opinions. The best managers know how to use praise as a motivator. They don't praise people too much or insincerely. They communicate by listening as well as talking.

If the employee has failed in performance, be sure to ask or point out what was done right. Ask the employee: "what good came from this experience or what have you learned from this?" or "How can you turn this to our advantage?" Many organizations have been improved because of the way managers and employees handled failure in a forthright manner of learning from failures and mistakes. These organizations have changed directions or methods, thus becoming more successful.

CREATE YOUR MOTIVATOR POSITION DESCRIPTION

It's time to create your own Motivator Position Description. Think about your position as a Motivator. What goals do you want to achieve? What can you do or say that is motivating to others?

MOTIVATOR POSITION DESCRIPTION

WHAT GOALS AND OBJECTIVES WOULD HELP YOU TO ACHIEVE A MOTIVATED TEAM?

1.

2.

3.

WHAT ACTIONS ARE YOU WILLING TO TAKE TO ACCOMPLISH THESE GOALS AND OBJECTIVES?

FOR GOAL 1:

1.

2.

3.

FOR GOAL 2:

1.

2.

3.

FOR GOAL 3:

1.

2.

3.

Often people are given assignments without an explanation of their responsibilities. With that in mind, we thought you might want to see an example of a MOTIVATOR POSITION DESCRIPTION:

MOTIVATOR POSITION DESCRIPTION

WHAT GOALS AND OBJECTIVES WOULD HELP YOU TO ACHIEVE A MOTIVATED TEAM?

1. Bring out each person's true potential for growth and development.

2. Motivate each team member to be more productive.

3. Identify what motivates each employee.

4. Determine what motivates me so that I can be a motivated leader for my team to follow.

WHAT ACTIONS ARE YOU WILLING TO TAKE TO ACCOMPLISH THESE GOALS AND OBJECTIVES?

FOR GOAL 1:

1. I will construct an Employee Development Plan with each of my employees for their growth and development.

2. I will hold a meeting, in which I will show my staff a detailed explanation of Maslow's Hierarchy of Needs. I will lead a group discussion to determine how their jobs help them to meet these needs. For those needs that aren't currently being met and are important, I will ask them to brainstorm ways to change the job or themselves in order to fulfill the needs.* Then decide how these can be applied to the client, customer, and public.

3. I will meet with each employee to discuss my initial thoughts and to plan an Employee Development Plan together.

Starting from the bottom of Maslow's Hierarchy of Needs, let's look at some of the responses of how people's needs are met by work.

Security Needs: Receiving the regular pay check and fringe benefits. The parking lot is well lighted at night and a security car drives through regularly. Video cameras are focused upon the parking lot.

Belonging or Social Needs: People make friends at work. They form cliques of comfort during and after hours. Without work, they wouldn't have met these people.

Self Esteem Needs: My name was typed upon the report as the originator. I was mentioned in the memo to the President. I received an award. Our team was recognized for our outstanding performance. My title makes me feel important. When I take on a new project, I feel good about myself.

Self Actualization Needs: I was encouraged to attend a seminar. I was given a book to read that relates to skill improvement. My boss talked to me about my career development needs. I can choose to create and adjust my own job description.

FOR GOAL 2:

1. I will make at least 2 contacts per day with each employee under my direct supervision.

2. Within conversations with an employee, I will verbalize his/her name to emphasize that I care. This should help him/her feel important as well as validate his/her existence.

3. I will ask each employee for suggestions and write these down while conversing.

FOR GOAL 3:

1. I will notice what subjects each employee talks about the most. This should be an indicator of what motivates him/her. I will examine it in respect to Maslow's Hierarchy of Needs.

2. Based upon my observations, I will use this information to say and act in such a way as to motivate them. I will use these clues to communicate in ways that will stimulate their interest. I will compile these observations and then conclude what I can do and say as a way of using this information.

3. I will check on my progress in using this information in two weeks. I will set aside some time to review my objectives from the previous action.

FOR GOAL 4:

1. I will determine what or who demotivates me. I will notice when I feel deflated and try to determine why.

2. I will notice what sparks my interest or pushes my hot button. I will try to build more of those kinds of activities and thoughts into my job.

3. While driving to work, I will do things that put me in a happy frame of mind. I will allow myself extra time to get to work especially on rainy days. I will listen to relaxing music, inspirational messages or humor. I will watch what I am listening to and decide if this the type of attitude I want to create within myself. I know that what I listen to will create new thoughts and, ultimately, new actions. **

** An essential element of being a Motivator is preparation for each day as if it were a battle to be won over the forces of negative thinking. By listening to positive songs or tapes, you can actually prepare yourself to think positively and usually have a better day. One Motivator stated she never reads the paper in the morning because the newspapers are so negative. At the breakfast table with the family or spouse, project pleasantness rather than criticizing each other.

It should be noted that this Motivator chose to work on one goal for three weeks prior to continuing to the next goal.

TEN SPECIAL ISSUES THAT MAKE THE DIFFERENCE

1. GOAL SETTING AS A MOTIVATIONAL TOOL

It's important to set up incremental goals for your people. Rather than setting herculean tasks for the person, it's more effective to plan smaller activating steps or indicators along the way. These small indicators can serve as motivational steps so the person can see and feel a sense of accomplishment. You as a manager will need to analyze what those indicators should be.

When you set goals, obviously the goals should be as realistic as you can determine with limited information. Sometimes that is hard because so many variables can affect the outcome. If you don't meet your originally set goals, keep them the same or lower them somewhat. By no means make them higher. Nothing can be more discouraging than knowing you didn't meet your original goals and now you have to reach higher ones.

2. CARING ABOUT YOUR PEOPLE

Another aspect of the Motivator position description is being the type of leader that your people need you to be. You may want to do an ongoing needs assessment of your work force. This would entail everything that is of concern to your employees. From time to time you will be asking them how you can make life more comfortable for them or what problems you might be able to help them with.

For example, if a person has an aggravation and needs your help to correct it because it is beyond his/her control and authority, dealing with it promptly will earn points with your staff. Even if you can't correct it, this is saying to your employee, "I cared enough about your needs to put myself out on the line for you." This type of demonstration of concern about the work environment or willingness to make the job more pleasant communicates what you think is the value of your employees.

You might want to ask your employees what problems they are having with equipment, other people, or the general work area that you could help them with. For example a machine that repeatedly breaks down. Consider looking at certain purchases as investments rather than detriments. One employee told us how she would go to a new job and look around at the equipment and then sell her boss on buying new equipment so productivity could be improved rather than waiting for the equipment to be fixed. So often we forget to look at the tools until they are broken down beyond repair. Workers in plants are often concerned about that. They want to be able to work with good tools. Safety issues, too, must be dealt with immediately because they are basic to the well being of the employees.

3. THE REWARDING PROCESS AS A MOTIVATOR

Reward at increments as well as at the end of a project or month. In certain jobs, there can be numerous tasks being performed at the same time, but at different stages of development. Many times they really don't seem to finish their work because there are so many tasks. As a manager/supervisor you need to break down the work into smaller goals so people can have a sense of accomplishment along the way. Doing it on a daily or weekly basis can help achieve this.

A company in Wisconsin rewards their employees each month according to their performance. These employees receive small monetary bonuses. It's one more way to connect the pay with the work that has been done.

Another organization rewards its employees with free dinners for the employee and spouse and with trips to local events and amusement parks. The executives in that organization have found that involving the employee's family in the reward boosts the impact of the motivational reward.

Additional executive perks should be considered for hard working executives. These could include dinner in a foreign country or a long weekend in Europe with the spouse. Many companies now do this under the guise of business trips.

As an executive of a company, you may want to change your bonus pay structure somewhat to give incremental pay increases instead of the yearly bonus. Often it isn't a matter of the amount, but it's the thought behind it. If the thought is sincerely wishing to express appreciation, you've gone a long way to motivate and by the way, it's worth every penny of it.

Governmental executives, managers and supervisors have an even bigger challenge to think of motivational rewards for their people. With creative imaginations and time to brain storm, they have been able to develop rewards such these and others. The others include personal memos sent to the employee's home, memos placed in the employee's personnel file, private parties to reward the employee and his/her family, flowers or small gifts and recognition in front of peers and superiors.

4. JOB INVOLVEMENT

Essentially, we are suggesting some new concepts relating to job involvement.

Look around at your employees and ask yourself what would help them? Identify and examine their needs and then strategize ways to meet their needs. In the human service business, you take a case by case approach by specifically planning what will develop this person. Management can do the same thing by actually writing a plan for development for their people. Part of that is deciding what they will do for their employees' development.

The following is an example of just such a plan:

EMPLOYEE DEVELOPMENT PLAN FOR _____

1. WHAT ARE YOUR CURRENT EXPECTATIONS OF THIS PERSON?

2. LIST TEN STRENGTHS OF THIS EMPLOYEE:

3. BASED UPON THESE STRENGTHS, WHAT ADDITIONAL EXPECTATION(S) COULD YOU HAVE OF THIS PERSON?

4. WHAT WOULD BE YOUR FONDEST DREAM OF POTENTIAL FOR THIS PERSON?

5. WHAT COULD YOU DO TO ENCOURAGE HIM OR HER IN THIS DIRECTION?

6. WHAT ARE SOME BEHAVIORAL OBJECTIVES YOU CAN MAKE TO OBTAIN THESE EXPECTATIONS? THINK ABOUT MONTHLY, WEEKLY SPECIFIC ACTIVITIES THAT YOU COULD DO.

5. IT'S NEVER TOO SOON TO START THE MOTIVATIONAL PROCESS BY COMMUNICATING

Communicating with your employees is an important element of productive team development.

A pivotal motivational point is the orientation stage for a new employee. Instead of communicating that the job is really easy and quickly boring, the first line supervisor who communicates the fun parts and the challenging aspects to this new employee is creating a much more positive perspective. If a certain level of quality is demanded, the first line supervisor can show the employee how to get that. Then, when the new employee achieves a certain level of quality, the wise supervisor gets excited. We have seen too many people who have been eager for praise become stifled by the supervisor who criticizes instead of getting excited. Even if you are not the type of person to ahow excitement, go out of your way to produce some. This is a key point with your employees, so act excited and the feeling will come later.

As a supervisor, you have an obligation to learn the various aspects of your workers' jobs and to identify the most interesting or challenging parts.

You may even want to tell your employees that you're open to hearing about new ways to improve the job and its procedures. Olga Holden, Director of Human Resources and Planning, noted "People know when you're open to ideas and suggestion...you seek them out, you put them in charge of things.

You have to assess their capabilities and be really clear about what it is you want."

If you direct your employees' attention to improving the process or the quality of their efforts by asking questions and getting them to think about improving, you have begun to challenge them. One of the underlying concepts of implementing Statistical Process Control in manufacturing is that the process can always be improved and the worker on the line can be part of that improvement process. The underlying motivational impact can be tremendous, if the supervisors and middle management support the concepts by acting appropriately to employee suggestions and recommendations.

Employees who are encouraged to ask questions such as "How can I do this more efficiently and how can I do this better?" usually are interested in their work and discover they are no longer residing in coffins. No matter how many times you do a job, there is always something new to learn about it. Seeing the old job with new eyes that question will bring excitement. Every job can be exciting.

Making some kind of contact with the person is essential to keeping their motivational level up. A manager or supervisor can do this by sending a memo, talking face to face, by telephone, or in group meetings with 3 or 4 people.

One manager sent a thank you note to each employee at home. She wrote it on her personal stationary. The employees' families were able to give them recognition as well so it became a double pat on the back.

A supervisor at a hospital found it difficult to communicate with all of her employees because they worked three shifts and there was a sizable number of them. However, she was able send a personalized note of thanks through their mail boxes.

Managers need to create Contact Points with their employees. A Contact Point is a face to face, verbal or nonverbal interaction with an employee. It may be a smile or a hand shake. A Contact Point could also be having a cup of coffee with an employee and talking about work and nonwork related topics. The contact gives the person a positive stroke that may be needed. Each day, write on your calendar how many Contact Points you created. At the end of the week, figure out the number of Contact Points you've accumulated. Reward yourself for your performance.

6. WHAT'S YOUR MOTIVATIONAL EMPHASIS IN MEETINGS?

To keep people motivated, the emphasis of meetings should be upbeat and of a positive vein. Be sure to spend a significant amount of time on what has been accomplished. Secondly, when you want improvement, discuss it from the point of view: "Here's what we need to do in this area...." rather than "We shouldn't do this...." Notice the difference? The former phrase suggests positive action that will accomplish something, while the latter reinforces the negative and doesn't suggest what should be done.

One sales manager decided to spark his sales people's motivational level by asking them to write all their achievements as a team during the previous month. Then he wrote the achievements on a flip chart as the employees stated them. Then he reviewed the list with them by saying..."Wow, look at all that we have accomplished. That's really exceptional and especially recognizing what we had to go through to get there. Are you proud of yourselves? Well, you should be. I'm proud of you. You're a terrific group of people who always are in there trying. I'm really pleased. I believe we can go out and do the same or better this next month."

7. NOW FOR THOSE TOUGH NUTS: HERE'S HOW TO CRACK THEM

We've asked managers with employees that they disliked to write at least three characteristics that they could like. The report from the managers is very similar: it was difficult to do at first but they found it helped them to respond in a better fashion with the employees. It helped them to change their attitudes about these particular employees.

Everyone has something good about them even it's of a physical nature.

One word of caution for the manager, there are many types of motivational styles as we've discussed. Be careful not to classify someone as unmotivated just because they are not excited when you think they should be. It may take them longer to warm up in the morning or to a particular project. If the physical clues are not there, check on the results of their work. Does it look like they are enjoying it, putting in a full measure of effort and doing a good job?

For the employee who seems to be undermotivated, there is probably still something inside him/her that desires to make the work count for something, but unfortunately it feels useless from his/her perspective. If we were to ask, he or she would probably say something or someone is hampering his/her motivational level from rising. There may also be something happening in his/her personal life that stifles enthusiasm for work.

For some employees the work day resembles a coffin they enter to complete their requirements to live their lives. Another popular concept is the prison concept which is one of biding their time until they're free for retirement. When people perceive their lives after work as the most important part of their lives, they are wasting a tremendous amount of their lives. So are their organizations. How sad this is for them and their organizations. Both are losers. An undermotivated worker is a drain on profits, morale, productivity and a terrible waste of human potential. A past television commercial showed people entering jail cells with their business suits and working behind bars. Here's a question we've asked ourselves: What is it that creates a perspective that work is a jail cell and the time after work is really life? Is it an illusion or a perception? Is it a matter of control? Is it because people are on their own time? Why do these people shut themselves off for eight hours of their lives each day. How can this coffin be turned into a fine restaurant of work activities?

Partial answers to these questions appear in the statements, employees or their acquaintances make about their work. People say to each other on a occasion: "I wouldn't want to do your job." This unconsciously horrible statement is really a psychological insult. It strikes at the person's heart because at a social level, the statement is "I couldn't do what you do because of the sacrifices" and at psychological level it says "Uck! I wouldn't want to do what you do."

Sometimes these people haven't been challenged to produce beyond what they normally give. By settling for security, they have lost the incentive to see their work as important. Perhaps they are undermotivated because they don't see themselves moving ahead in the organization. They find work boring and the sameness has set in. This type of employee becomes a real challenge to motivate because you're fighting social mores that say work should not be exciting. Too many people think life owes them excitement. When the reverse is true, people make life exciting for themselves. One Motivator told us her perspective, "Whether you have a good day or not depends upon your perception and your willingness to laugh and enjoy every part of the job."

Every job has an interesting or rewarding part to it. When both the employee and the manager/supervisor lose sight of this fact, there is a greater potential for producing an undermotivated employee. The manager needs to help them see what the benefits of their jobs are.

Try to find out what motivates them. Try hard for at least a year to get them going.

There are the dead heads in zombie bodies walking around with no motivation. These people seemingly were forced into this life. They don't want to be here and they certainly don't want to work or do anything. With a dead head, he/she needs to recognize self worth and gain a higher sense of self esteem. If you can't turn them around, you are better off terminating their employment than pushing them off on another part of the company or to another organization.

Cautionary note here: be sure when you determine someone is unmotivated, that you haven't projected your vision of what or how he/she should be doing or acting. Some people don't act motivated but still accomplish their work. Consider how he/she acts after work, if there is a strong interest, then you have a clue that he/she can be motivated. If he/she seems motivated after work, talk about what motivates him/her after work.

A natural event in the downward motivational spiral is the proclivity of the manager to concentrate on the hopelessness of the problem rather than on the belief it can be solved and concentrate on the common bonds between the manager and the employee.

To determine ways you could improve your management skills, consider doing exit interviews with employees leaving of their own accord. Asking what were some of the problems that perhaps demotivated people can provide valuable information. In an exit interview a person can say how he/she would like to have been treated. Ask what types of motivational responses he/she would have liked from the organization.

8. USING POWER AND RESOURCES WISELY

Regarding power, a management person is almost always better off not to exercise power. The knowledge that someone has power is usually a stronger motivator than actually using it. Some individuals believe that exercising power is the best way to achieve results, when a far easier and more effective method exists. Desire is a very strong motivator and a longer lasting one than fear. The other side of it is desire is easier to control than fear. By giving up tight control over everything, the manager/supervisor gains the best type of control. This control asks and expects only the best from every employee with the promise of a frequent reward.

Fear, exercising power and closely overseeing many details create children of adults, deflate productivity, lower potential profits and limit achievements.

The pertinent principle is recognizing that people are really resources. We need to see people as living resources instead of seeing them mechanistically as bodies laboring or filling spaces on the organizational chart. With the perception that they can contribute to the organization through their valuable ideas and inputs. With the way professional people have moved from organization to organization, organizations need to tap these resource early with positive motivational team building approaches.

The Japanese have shown us that there are other ways to beneficially use their human resources to create quality products, thus improving productivity, and ultimately increasing the long range profits. Instead of milking the cow dry, they leave the cow alive for another day. If you help people achieve their needs and desires, they will give out their best for you.

In interviewing Motivators, we have found the best managers are those who care about their people. Their turnover rates are lower, productivity is higher and profits from the team's efforts are always rising.

At the other extreme, is an example of a manager of a production department,who rules with an iron fist. His people take their full allotment of sick days, vacation time and generally work hard only while he's watching. At this point, he has been able to meet his quotas, but through the use of fear. People try to get out of his department as quickly as possible. Unfortunately, the owners of the company are not yet aware that he could produce even more, if he ran a more effective department by taking care of his people.

Using human resources wisely also means providing a motivational climate. Motivation is getting people to want to do something. Working is really a matter of perception. Working is a priviledge. Each job has a rewarding side to it.

9. TWO WAY MOTIVATION

Everyone from the top of an organization to the bottom likes to hear about the good job they've done or what is good about them, personally. All too often, top management doesn't hear about what they've done right and how others in the company appreciate their efforts. If you're an employee, supervisor or middle manager, ask yourself this question: "When was the last time I said something positive about this company to an executive or a manager a level above me in the organizational chart?" Do it today. Watch the result. Surprise them by not asking for anything after you make the comment. You can just finish by saying: "I just thought you might like to know."

Everyone needs to hear positive aspects about themselves or their work. You can motivate your boss by just such a simple action. We have heard many managers and supervisors say or infer that they don't feel appreciated by their employees. One manager commented that his people forgot to say thanks for helping them get their pay check problems resolved by pay day.

10. MOTIVATION IS REWARDING

The benefits of working around motivated people consist of numerous qualitative and quantitative measures. The best managers experience these benefits every day. Motivated managers are often surrounded by motivated employees. These managers find their jobs exciting and enjoyable. The motivation spreads to other areas of their lives: family life, church, community, and service clubs. This carry over benefit is rooted in that motivation is a life skill as well as a job skill. This enhancement is a direct result of motivation. Great managers have learned that their satisfaction no longer comes from doing the work as much as it comes from seeing their people accomplishing the work with their support, advice, leadership and motivational enthusiasm. They know they have created the environment for their people to be motivated to work hard. Managers' rewards are motivated employees.

Motivating is fun! You'll find yourself smiling more when you are motivating others. In some ways it's like playing Santa Claus year round because you're making others and yourself happier by giving the gift of motivation. You will discover the joy of giving because of how your people are responding. You have fewer problems because they want to do their best. The days of carrots and sticks are gone. Carrots work for awhile and sticks far less. Who said work was drugery? Who said we have to push people or they won't work? Motivated people don't have to be pushed, they want to move ahead.

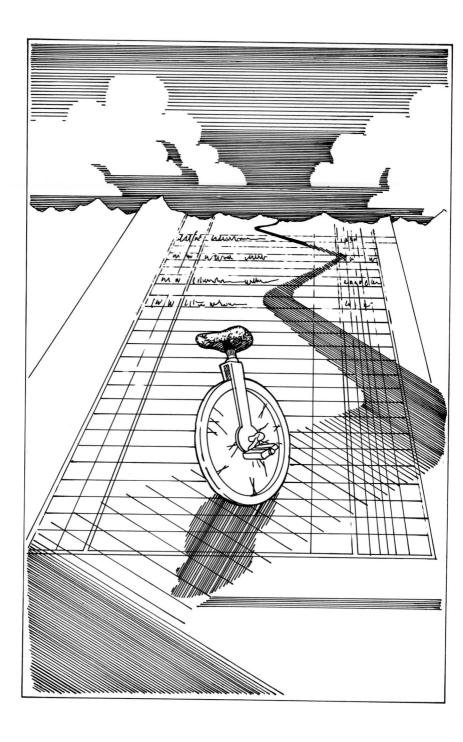

C-3
HARNESSING THE POWER FOR BOTTOM LINE SUCCESS

Certainly, management's conclusions are changing regarding who and what motivates people. In this period of transition between money being considered the primary motivator and the intangible aspects gaining more importance, all levels of management have begun to ask what truly motivates people? During the writing of this book an employee of a major manufacturer said to one of the authors, "you don't get motivated by working for THIS COMPANY." Another employee standing around with us, quickly said, "I'm motivated by my work." Each had a valid opinion based upon their perspectives, experiences and values. If you were the manager of both these men, you would want to find out what intangibles motivated them. So it is with all levels of management, the key to a company's success is motivated people. Ah, but what and how?

If we are to compete with the best of the world's work forces, we need to be able to change our management motivational styles. Past statistics of business' failures indicate motivation has a dollar value attached to it. Further, corporations are noticing that management styles can affect productivity and profits. As a nation based upon capitalism, a catalyst is needed to move corporations and even nonprofit organizations in this direction of exploring how people are motivated. That catalyst is the loss of market share to foreign companies and changing budget considerations.

Where else can we make such great strides? We've certainly improved the art of doing business tremendously in the technological and financial management areas over the last twenty five years.

We have a fantastic opportunity to work with the remaining area that can be LIMITLESS in potential: the people area. It's the least predictable but CAN BE the most beneficial in the long run.

With the technological changes, we've had to adapt, but have we given enough and the appropriate kind of attention to social progress? Probably not. Every management level within America's corporations needs to consider how to give more to the people needs because of the technological changes and to gain even greater productivity.

Simply stated it's the care and feeding of the people. It's a well documented fact that machines that are well maintained last longer. Relationships that continue to be developed also last longer. Some management employee relationships have been treated with less care than some machines.

The companies that show that they care, get what they want from their people very willingly! People give out tremendous energy when there is a clear cut purpose, a known reward or sense of fulfillment and they have made a conscious commitment to the goals. Top management of the companies that know this secret to motivation, structure themselves formally and informally to provide employees with purposes for projects and the promise of rewards. They ask for commitments, not just once but thousands of times on big and little projects. The result: their motivated people produce exponentially more than the undermotivated people of the competition.

The way the world is changing and the way people are changing, new motivational strategies are needed. Motivated people are known to produce. Motivation is worth money. Undermotivated people are a drain upon a company. People who are highly motivated make the difference in profit margins. There is a direct link between motivation and productivity. It has been difficult to strictly identify that relationship in the past. However, managers have increasingly become aware as technology changes, people also need to change and be prepared to not only accept change but readily create it.

NEW MOTIVATION DEVELOPMENTS

People in certain areas are working harder and taking responsibility for the quality of their work. One example was related by an auto worker who is a team leader in a plant practicing motivational principles. He described how his team worked together and were very flexible to the needs of the cars coming in. When one part of the team was overloaded another part of the team would shift over and help them. The supervisor meets with the team regularly. When the team requested that they all be given overtime versus a few having to stay, the supervisor agreed. The net result: the next time the supervisor needed their help, he had their support. This supervisor has learned that people will respect him because he listens and admits he doesn't know everything.

That's an example of how people can be motivated. A wise person once said that people will give to you what you want if you give them what they want. Where teams start working together, people become motivated and produce quality.

The cottage industry is evolving as an integral part of corporations in America not as a separate entity as it was originally conceived. People are able to have two offices, one at home which they use part of the week with their computers tied in to the headquarter's main computers. These same people are often spread out throughout the company. The extended office requires special management skills to keep the relationships alive and well. Phone and computer contact replace face to face communication. People are far too social to become islands without communication. In fact some people have commented that this type of communication can be preferable because the time on the phone is concentrated. The time spent communicating is a more quality time for some, however for others it can aggravate an already poor communication relationship.

Being away from the group can create a new need for interaction with others. Today, we take for granted the interactions we have all the time. You only need to talk to a person who has just started to work in a home office a short time to realize how much he or she misses the social part of the work group. Working with others is a motivator for many people.
Communication about work and occupational craziness can be enjoyable and motivational. It provides a psychological stroke that is very necessary for most people.

HARNESSING THE POWER

More and more managers and supervisors are learning that they can become even more effective by cashing in on their people's expertise and common sense. They only momentarily lose power. The type of power that is lost is the autocratic position power, when this is given up, they gain influence and charismatic power. Given a choice between the two, the wise leaders choose the latter hands down.

Most people want to do the best job that they can. They get discouraged when people or politics get in the way of doing a good job. Managers in manufacturing companies are slowly realizing that the people closest to the work can often make the best decisions about how to do the work.

Those of us in Corporate America have an unique opportunity to develop ourselves and develop those around us. We said in the beginning of this book that everyone has the power to motivate himself or herself. As executives, managers and supervisors, we can use our power to motivate or demotivate our employees. By using the power positively, the expandable resource expands. By choosing to use the power negatively, this expandable resource shrinks as do savings and profits. Motivation is no longer just a nice concept to consider in management seminars. It is a necessity to realize your power to motivate if you are to survive the future. If you can harness your power to motivate yourself and others, you have the magic to create bottom line success.

For More Information About Consultation, Seminars, and Quantity Orders For Books, Contact

Milestones Unlimited
Suite 105
35552 Grand River Avenue
Farmington Hills, Michigan 48024

(313) 477-9555